Journey-Work of the Stars

An Astrology Workbook

Rosanne Finn

ISBN 978-0-9997087-0-5

To obtain additional copies of this book or
for Astrological Services and Classes with Rosie Finn:

www.astrologywithrosiefinn.com

Copyright © 2018   Rosanne Finn

Ask permission before reprinting any part of this book.

Cover art by Rosanne Finn

Dedicated to all my dear friends who have supported me in my work.

A big hug of gratitude for Carol Trasatto, whose presence, loyalty, and wisdom are a treasure in my life. A deep bow for Marie Poland whose enthusiasm, encouragement and support have gotten me out ruts many times. A candle lit for Shari Trnka whose vision, understanding and witnessing have kept me inspired. Thank you to Carol and Marie for doing the painstaking work of editing. Thank you to my son, Finn Greiner, for simply being you in my life.

Table of Contents

Introduction 9
The Elements 12
The Modalities 15
The Signs of the Zodiac 19
The Planets 37
   The Symbols 39
Rulerships 79
The Houses 81
Putting the Planet, Sign and House Together 93
The Angles 99
Aspects 103
   Finding Aspects in a Chart 112
   Multiple Aspect Patterns 114
The Phases of the Moon 119
Declinations 122
Transits 123
The Ephemeris 125
Progressions 127
Postscript 131
Resources 140
Glossary 142

I believe a leaf of grass is no less than the journey-work of the stars,
And the prismire is equally perfect, and a grain of sand, and the egg of the wren,
And the tree-toad is a chef-d'oeuvre for the highest,
And the running blackberry would adorn the parlors of heaven,
And the narrowest hinge in my hand puts to scorn all machinery,
And the cow crunching with depress'd head surpasses any statue,
And a mouse is miracle enough to stagger sextillions of infidels.[1]

from Song of Myself, Verse 31, by Walt Whitman

This is a workbook to introduce you to the art and science of astrological interpretation. I see astrology as an art and a science—the art of seeing a beautiful picture of symbols and geometry and speaking its form into existence and the science of collecting and analyzing the data and geometry that accompanies every chart. With astrology, we look into the heavens, the macro-scope, in order to glean insight into the micro-scope of our lives. We take patterns and forms and put language to them. We watch with awe as an apparently chaotic representation of the placement of celestial bodies begins to take shape into a spiraling pattern that repeats itself over and over again as we dig deeper and deeper into layer upon layer of truth.

The magic that a chart offers is always new to me. Every chart is perfect. Every moment has meaning. I have never seen a chart, a celestial reflection of the moment, which did not have depth, soul, and beauty. For me, the work of astrology has been a gift the Universe gave to me so that I could see each person as whole, each person as perfect, as a growing living being deserving of respect, comfort and compassion.

For us to see the gifts of a chart and the beauty in a chart, we must slip out of dualistic thinking, out of the dogma and the rote interpretations that limit and trap the being connected to the chart. It has been my attempt with this workbook to offer an accumulation of material that offers a way of thinking about the planets, signs and houses that does not limit our experience, but opens us up to seeing who we are and the circumstances of our lives through the unique lens of astrology.

Most of the workbook is simply the basics, put into one document. I encourage you to gather over time the resources that I have listed, since they offer explanations in much greater depth.

I hope that this book is a help and inspiration to you in your journey-work and that I have conveyed my respect and gratitude for the art and science of astrology.

Blessings,
Rosie Finn

---

[1] Walt Whitman. *Leaves of Grass and Selected Prose.* [Rutland, VT: 1993, Everyman's Library] from "Song of Myself", Verse 31.

8

Introduction

An Introduction to the "Work" of Astrology

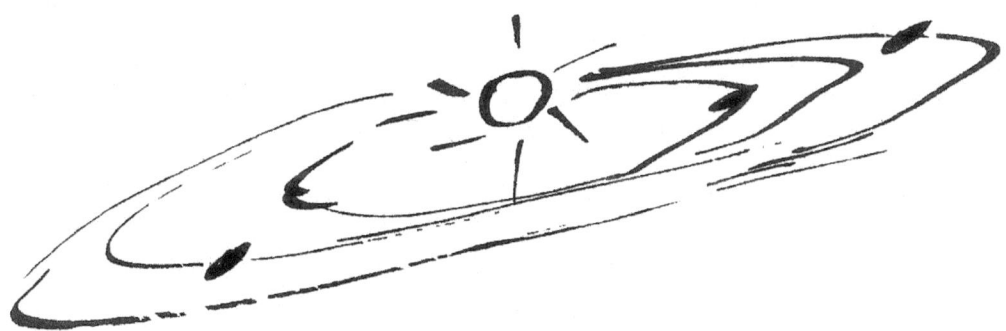

In something we call science there are two forms of energy: potential and kinetic. Potential energy is energy waiting to be used and kinetic energy is energy in use (my own definitions). "Work" is what is required in order to move energy from potential to kinetic, "work" being a technical scientific term complete with an equation. By the term "work", we mean the transfer of energy between two bodies.[2] I think these definitions are helpful for us in looking at how best to use astrology. The "work" of astrology is the transfer of energy from ignorance to awareness, from stagnation to positive flow, from karma to dharma.

There are many ways for this work to happen; astrology is simply one way. One use of astrology is for prediction—a way of looking at patterns and projecting the pattern into the future. This is a helpful way if what we are looking for is a better way of planning and having control in our lives. Yet, astrology can also be a mechanism for the actual transfer of energy—in much the same way meditation, yoga, sacred geometry, dance, and many other forms transform us through practicing. As in sacred geometry, the very experience of the view is the path for transferring energy—or transformation. Meditation transforms us in the minute we sit and breathe. Astrology, too, is a transformative experience as we study, witness and interpret.

---

[2] Nolan, Peter J. *Fundamentals of College Physics*. [New York: SUNY at Farmingdale, NY, 1993, Brown Publishers] p. 566

Introduction

When I work with astrology, the consciousness of a person is an undeterminable factor from simply looking at the chart, although I know there are many who would disagree with me and they may be correct. For now, though, let's keep it as an unknown. This unknown quotient is the ability of a person to transfer energy—or to transform. The greater the view, the more able we are to transfer energy—partly because we can see where the potential exists and how to move it to where it is best served. The perspective serves our ability to "work". Someone once told me a quote from a very wealthy Indian guru living in America. Someone asked the guru where they were going to get the money for some such project or other and the guru responded, "From wherever it is." When we have a large enough perspective, we can see where the energy is for us to use—whether the energy is in the form of money, time, physical resources, strength, love, kindness or patience.

When we look at an astrology chart, we see the location of the planets in relationship to each other and to space—the stars, the galaxy, and beyond. Whether we use the tropical zodiac or the sidereal zodiac, we are looking at the mapping of space. The tropical zodiac places great importance on the tilt of our planet and the altered perspective we get from that. It aligns with the seasons and holds our relationship to earth as sacred. The sidereal zodiac holds the stars as our orientation and fixes us in space in relationship to the stars. Both methods are mapping the planets in relation to space and to the actual placement of the planets. If we are working directly with the movement of the planets in relation to each other and to the stars and the galaxies, which zodiac does not matter—only that we align our intuition with the tool that we are using.

I often hear people get stuck in the use of the signs of the zodiac—my moon is in Scorpio therefore I am always going to be such and such. While this way of using astrology may be supportive at times, I find its limitations stifling. The planets are always in motion—always relating to each other in different angles and different speed relations. We are always evolving, even when it seems we are not. To devolve as a human being is a rare and tragic thing. For our purposes, let's hold that we are all evolving, all becoming more conscious, learning and growing.

~~~~~~~~~~~~~~~~

If we were sitting on the Sun, the planets would seem to move forward at fairly constant speeds, spinning at fairly constant rotational speeds, moving in and out of angles once and moving on at the same pace. As we sit on Earth, the planets sometimes appear to move backwards, sometimes make the same angle back and forth three, five and sometimes even seven times. It's like on the Sun, one time—Pow! On Earth, we need a few passes to get it. Thank goodness the Universe gives us that.

It is these movements and angular relationships that give us the ability to use planetary mapping as a tool for increasing awareness. If we look at the chart as stagnant then we miss the ability to use it to its full potential.

As we begin to look at how to witness the movement and relations of the planets to each other, we begin a journey that has meaning. As humans in these amazing bodies at this time, we have consciousness to create our own mythology—our own stories. We are not bound to the stories of the past—nor do I think that those writing those stories ever expected them to become stagnant.

As we do this work together, we are absorbing and aligning with the movement of the planets so that we increase our perspective. The more we know and see the energy patterns of our solar system, the better equipped we are to ride the waves of the particular purposes of this lifetime.

Introduction

Overview of Planets, Signs and Houses

Planet	Planet Description	Sign	Sign Description	House	House Description
Mars	action; behavior; drive; personal will; ability to assert oneself	Aries	spontaneously; impulsively; fearlessly; instinctively	1st	self; the persona; physical appearance; identity; personality
Venus	magnetism; ability to attract what you want; artistic ability; creativity; human love	Taurus	confidently; slowly; with certainty; persistently	2nd	values; resources; money; investments
Mercury	communication; how we learn and think; oral and written expression; language	Gemini	curiously; flexibly; with interest; with versatility	3rd	immediate surroundings; communication; siblings; neighbors
Moon	feelings; how we feel nurtured; how we process input	Cancer	sensitively; with care; emotionally; with nurturance; tenaciously	4th	home; foundations; nature of one's domestic life; family; roots
Sun	the essence; vitality; radiance; who we truly are	Leo	boldly; powerfully; passionately; with self-assurance	5th	self-expression; creativity; children; play; recreation
Chiron	healing; connection between known and unknown	Virgo	clearly; concisely; with attention and focus; cleanly; honestly	6th	service; health; our path of incarnation into a body; daily routines; pets
Juno	partnership; commitment	Libra	diplomatically; with justice and a sense of fairness	7th	partnership; marriage; business relationships
Pluto	transformation; death; rebirth; evolution	Scorpio	intensely; deeply; absorbing and processing emotions	8th	sexuality; death; transformation; our ancestors; rebirth
Jupiter	expansion; growth; search for knowledge and truth; vision	Sagittarius	generously; optimistically; with vision; socially; abundantly	9th	travel; exploration; philosophy; higher education; seeking
Saturn	contraction; manifestation; creating form; reality; vocation	Capricorn	seriously; realistically; with integrity; with boundaries	10th	life path; vocation; dharma; what the world wants from us
Uranus	change; sudden unexpected shifts; aliveness; awakeness	Aquarius	eccentrically; radically; innovatively; collectively	11th	community; friends; gatherings; the future
Neptune	Connection to spirit; mystery; vision; divine love	Pisces	compassionately; kindly; perceptively; imaginatively	12th	completions; karma; endings; dissolutions; solitude; spirituality

The Elements

In order to understand the signs of the Zodiac, we must first understand the Elements and Modalities. The twelve signs of the zodiac are divided by four (the elements) and by three (the modalities). Each sign has its own unique combination of element and modality. It is this combination that gives each sign its unique characteristics. The four elements are Fire, Earth, Air and Water. The three modalities are Cardinal, Fixed and Mutable.

	Fire	**Earth**	**Air**	**Water**
Cardinal	Aries	Capricorn	Libra	Cancer
Fixed	Leo	Taurus	Aquarius	Scorpio
Mutable	Sagittarius	Virgo	Gemini	Pisces

The four elements represent the four corners of life, the four directions and the four states of reality. Whenever we have something divided by four we will find some connection to the elements. I look at the elements as different ways of relating to life, four different perspectives. While we each are composes of all four elements, we may have leanings toward one or another. Dennis Klocek calls the elements "qualities describing the subtle interplay of forces". [3] It is considered that there are four forces in the universe, or at least in our third-dimensional world. There is *gravity*, or impedance, the strong force that ties us down or in or on. This is the Earth element. There is *electromagnetic* force, the energy that vibrates and awakens, the Fire element. There are the *weak* forces that loosely bind and include radioactive decay, the Air element. Lastly, there are the *strong* bonding forces that keep the nucleus together, that provide deep connection, the Water element.

Fire is the principle of action, ether and spirit. It is the essence of life. Temperature, which is now defined as simply the speed in which atoms and molecules interact, is related to fire. It is the principle of speed. The faster an atom moves, the more interaction, and the hotter it becomes. The heat is emitted from the speed of the interaction. Fire is the perspective: *We are all spirit. Anything is possible.*

Earth is the principle of beingness, of matter, of space, of solidity, of density, of reality. It is the art of "isness". It is the yogi in the lotus position, completely still. Earth is stillness, groundedness, connection to matter and the physical. Earth is crystallization, things taking form—a form that can be detected through the five senses. Earth is the perspective: *what you see, smell, taste, hear and feel is what you get.*

Air is the principle of thought, of communication, of idea, of understanding. All energy moves in spirals. Thought waves are spirals of energy that can interact with matter. Vibrations, frequency, waves are all air manifestations. Air is the perspective: *Our thoughts create our reality.*

---

[3] Klocek, Dennis. *A Biodynamic Book of Moons*. [Wyoming, RI: 1983, Bio-dynamic Literature].

The Elements

Water is the principle of connection, of feelings, of emotions, of love. Liquid moves in ways that solids cannot, bending and shaping itself to the forms around it, carrying waves of energy, and transforming everything in its path. Water is the perspective: *We are all interconnected with everything and one thing cannot change without changing everything else.*

FIRE	EARTH	AIR	WATER
heat	gravity	fusion	fission
activity	grounding	vibration	connection
creative	dense	light	cleansing
vision	touch	hearing	taste and smell
optimistic	practical	communicative	emotional
passion	sensuality	communication	emotion
joy	beauty	peace	love
a song or dance	a painting or sculpture	a book or poem	A film or play
I forgive you	Please forgive me	Thank you	I love you
Paul	Ringo	John	George
Spring	Winter	Fall	Summer
spirit	world	thought	emotion

The Elements

More ways of looking at the Elements:

	FIRE	**EARTH**	**AIR**	**WATER**
Tarot	Wands	Discs/Pentacles	Swords	Cups
Celtic	Spear	Stone	Sword	Cauldron
Jung	Intuition	Sensation	Thinking	Feeling
Direction	South	North	East	West
Phases	Plasma	Solid	Gas	Liquid
Gender	Masculine	Feminine	Masculine	Feminine
Wizard of Oz	Lion	Dorothy	Scarecrow	Tin Man
Seasons	Spring	Winter	Autumn	Summer
4 Aims in Life	Dharma	Artha	Kama	Moksha
4 Forces	Electromagnetism	Gravitation	Weak nuclear	Strong nuclear

The Modalities

The Modalities are related to the third harmonic and the number three. Three is a stable number whereby the three support each other without domination or stress. It is a number of strength. For instance, there are three fire signs—all of which support each other and are in harmony with each other. The three fire signs are divided into three different modalities; cardinal, fixed and mutable. This is the case with each of the elements. The modalities are related to the principle of Time.

Cardinal is the principle of initiation, of beginning, of the initial spark, desire, idea and conception. It is the act of creation.
It is the power of the element to begin; to initiate.
Power is unleashed and emerges with driving force.
It is centrifugal radiating energy; "action is a definite direction". Energy begins at the source and spirals in a plane outward.

Aries, Cancer, Libra and Capricorn are the Cardinal signs. Aries is the initiation of fire, the spark of creativity. Cancer is the birth of water, emotion that moves outward toward another. Libra is the initiation of air, the reaching out to connect. Capricorn is the construction of earth, the original plan.

Fixed is the principle of sustaining, of holding, of tending to, of perseverance. It is the act of existence.
The power of the element becomes concentrated.
Force is captured and rooted to one place.
It is centripetal energy (energy radiating inward toward a center), inertia, concentration, perseverance, here and now, pulling energy toward the center.

Taurus, Leo, Scorpio and Aquarius are the fixed signs. Taurus is the sustenance of earth, earth as it stabilizes. Leo is the holding of fire, a fire that burns bright and lasts long, like the fire in a temple. Scorpio is the holding of water, emotion as it goes deeper. Aquarius is the perseverance of air, the ability to think intellectually for long periods of time.

Mutable is the principle of adjustment, of going with the flow, of change, of alteration, of allowing, of accepting. It is the act of transformation.
The power of the element is dispersed.
Power spirals out taking various shapes.
Energy flows in a spiral column flexing and adjusting to the environment.

Gemini, Virgo, Sagittarius and Pisces are the mutable signs. Gemini is the adaptable air sign, mental flexibility. Virgo is the adaptable earth sign, the ability to adjust to physical changes. Sagittarius is the flexible fire sign, the ability to adapt to new inspiration. Pisces is the flowing water sign, the emotions flow through us.

The Modalities

Exercise: Meeting the Planets

Fill in the blanks from examining your birth chart.
For extra credit, use the symbols from the chart in Appendix B.
For a free copy of your chart, go to astro.com.

My _____ is in _____ ; element _____ modality _____.
  (planet)   (sign)

My _____ is in _____ ; element _____ modality _____.
  (planet)   (sign)

My _____ is in _____ ; element _____ modality _____.
  (planet)   (sign)

My _____ is in _____ ; element _____ modality _____.
  (planet)   (sign)

My _____ is in _____ ; element _____ modality _____.
  (planet)   (sign)

My _____ is in _____ ; element _____ modality _____.
  (planet)   (sign)

My _____ is in _____ ; element _____ modality _____.
  (planet)   (sign)

My _____ is in _____ ; element _____ modality _____.
  (planet)   (sign)

My _____ is in _____ ; element _____ modality _____.
  (planet)   (sign)

My _____ is in _____ ; element _____ modality _____.
  (planet)   (sign)

My _____ is in _____ ; element _____ modality _____.
  (planet)   (sign)

The Modalities

My _____ is in _____ ; element _____ modality _____.
   (asteroid)   (sign)

My _____ is in _____ ; element _____ modality _____.
   (asteroid)   (sign)

My _____ is in _____ ; element _____ modality _____.
   (asteroid)   (sign)

My _____ is in _____ ; element _____ modality _____.
   (asteroid)   (sign)

My _____ is in _____ ; element _____ modality _____.
   (North Node) (sign)

My _____ is in _____ ; element _____ modality _____.
   (South Node) (sign)

	Total Planets	Total Asteroids + Nodes		Total Planets	Total Asteroids + Nodes
Fire	_____	_____	Cardinal	_____	_____
Earth	_____	_____	Fixed	_____	_____
Air	_____	_____	Mutable	_____	_____
Water	_____	_____			

The Modalities

Describe the balance of the elements and modalities in your chart.
Do you have an excess or lack of an element?
Do you find your perspective on life relates to your elemental balance?

Example: If you have an abundance of planets in the Earth signs, do you tend to focus on what is right in front of you? If you have an abundance of air, do you find that your thoughts predominate any picture you have of reality? If you have an abundance of Fire, do you tend to be restless or easily agitated? If you have an abundance of Water, are you more sensitive or emotional, have a hard time separating out what are your feelings from others' feelings?

The Signs of the Zodiac

The twelve signs of the Zodiac form a circle that has no ending and no beginning. The
signs are basically a way of dividing the sky into twelve equal portions.
Each portion represents the energy of that part of the sky.
The signs carry the essence of the season in which the Sun roams through that sign.
We use the Sun and its apparent path around the Earth (called the *ecliptic*)
to set the stage for the signs.
The Sun travels for about a month in each sign.
This system is called the Tropical Zodiac.

There are other Zodiac systems. Another common Zodiac is the Sidereal Zodiac. The Sidereal Zodiac uses the constellations to separate the sky into 12 equal sections. This system is used more often in India in the Vedic system although it is gaining popularity in the West. While the Sidereal system may make more sense to scientists (this is the system astronomers use), we in the West tend to be somewhat out of touch with the stars and are much more focused on the Sun. Being a culture that worships the Hero which is a solar-based archetype and with all of our holidays based on the solar calendar, the Tropical Zodiac makes sense since it is a solar-based system. The Sidereal system is a more stellar-based system. Cultures that are more in touch with the rhythms of the moon and stars are more attuned to that system. Their holidays are based on the relationship between the Sun, the Moon and the rest of the sky.

The Remedy to the previous Zodiac sign's afflictions...

The Zodiac signs as stages in the life cycle of an organization...

The Zodiac signs as polarities...

| One way to look at the progression of the signs is that each sign is the answer to the previous sign's issues. Each sign has qualities that when taken to an extreme have undesirable effects. The following sign is the remedy to the deleterious side of the previous sign. | Another way to look at the signs is in relation to the development of a person, an organization, a relationship or a project of any kind. One can divide the cycle into twelve stages, look to the signs for understanding of each stage, and look to that stage for understanding the sign. | A third way to understand the signs is to look at the sign's opposite. Every sign has a polar sign. These two signs share the same modality but are of a different element. There are some qualities that are shared and some qualities that are naturally opposite. |

The Signs of the Zodiac

The Zodiac signs as polarities . . .

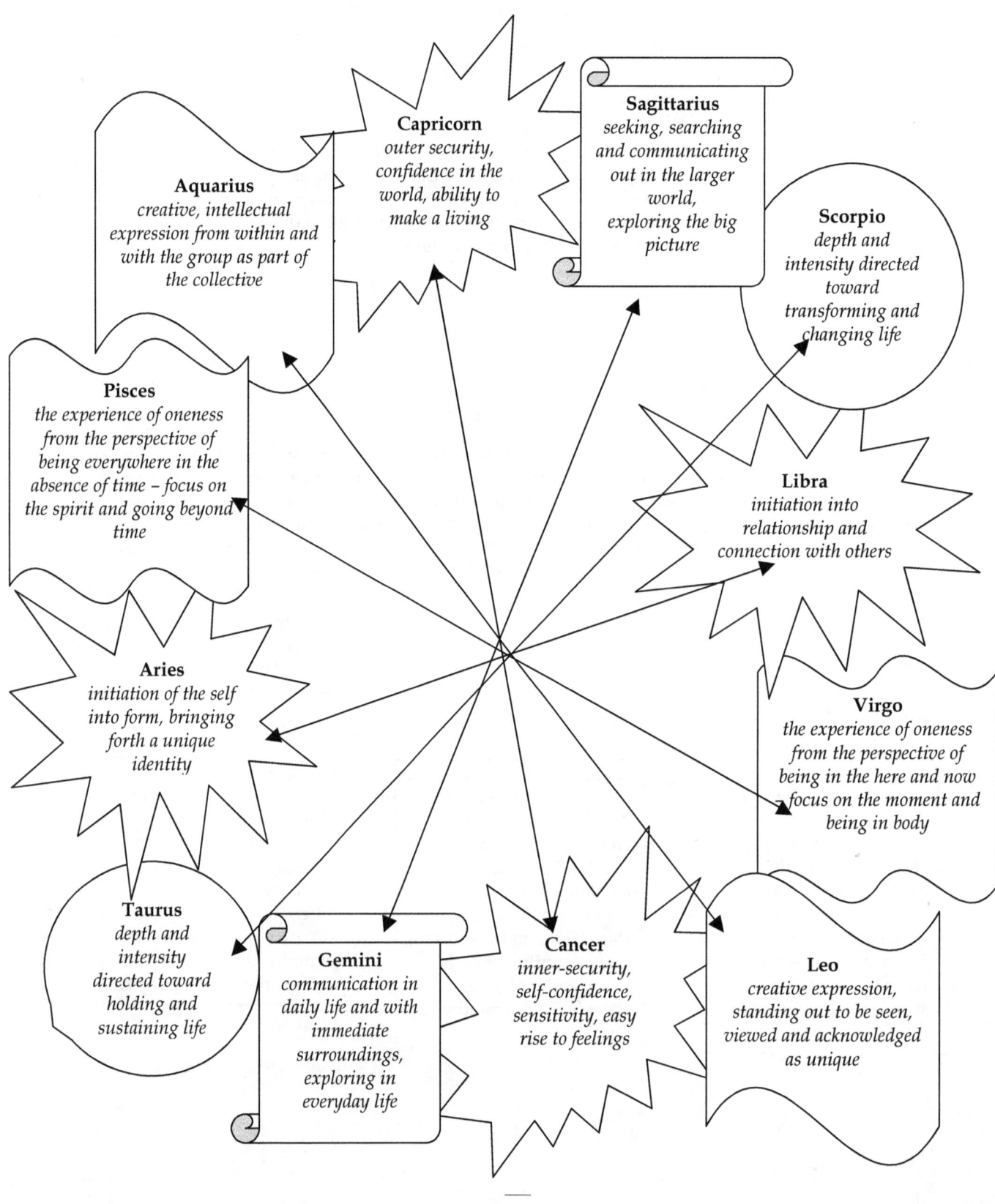

The Signs of the Zodiac

The Zodiac signs as stages in the life cycle of an organization.

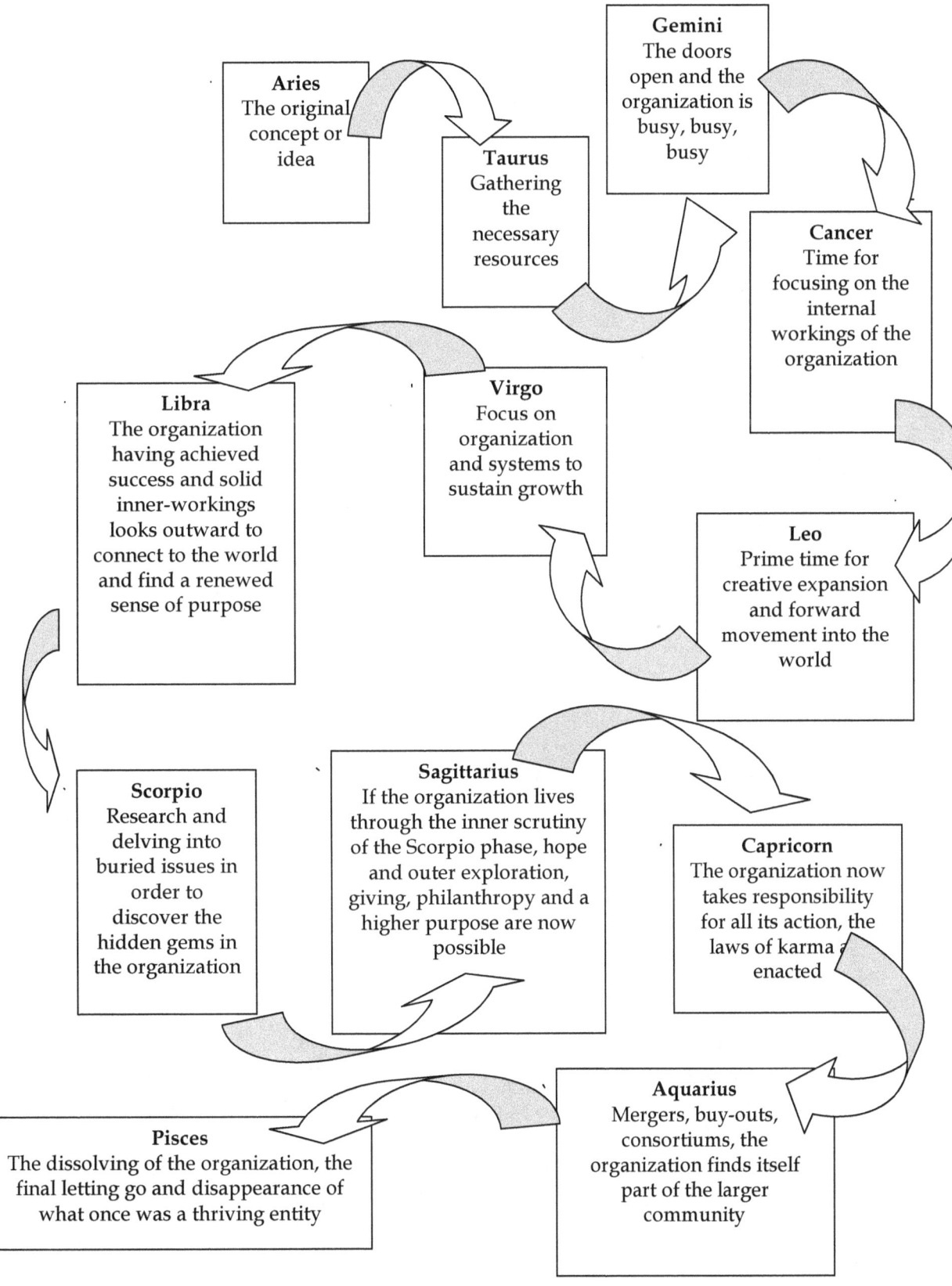

The Signs of the Zodiac

The Remedy to the previous sign's afflictions . . .

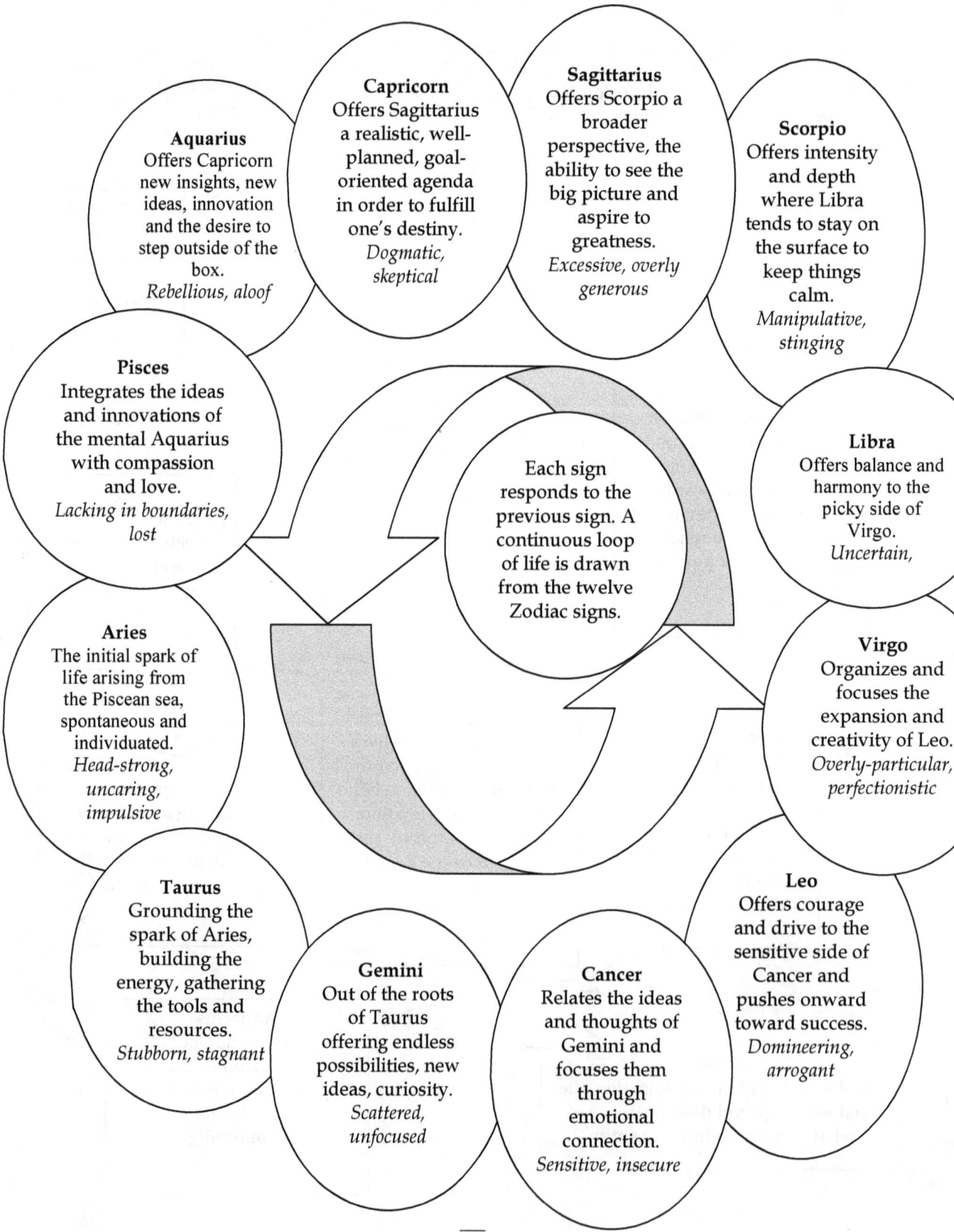

Aries

Planetary Ruler: Mars
Element: Fire
Modality: Cardinal

Body Part: Head, brain
Season: The beginning of spring

Archetype: The Ram
Mythology: The Search for a Separate Identity, Pallas Athene, Luke Skywalker

Aries is a sign of initiation, beginning and pure uninhibited self-expression. It is the spark of life, The Fool and courage. It is the urge to begin something for no reason other than it is the moment to do so. Pure spontaneous action is the Aries signature. A planet in Aries puts itself out into the world on the edge often without consideration of the circumstances. This planet will take risks and be daring. A planet in Aries will easily display itself and be seen for what it is. The planet in Aries may show extraordinary force of will—as if that planet must exert itself into the chart and characteristics of the native.

What to be aware of: The tendency of a planet in Aries to impulsively act without regard for consequences, a challenge in taking responsibility, and the ease in which anger, aggressiveness and impatience can be a response to the realities of life. When taken to an extreme, Aries can express itself rashly, without caring and impulsively without regard for circumstances.

Aries responds to Pisces by offering the spark of creativity, spontaneity, not caring what others think and helping Pisces find itself in that sea of oneness. Aries is the sign of the individual and helps us to individuate after the Cosmic Consciousness of Pisces.	**Aries: Birth** Aries is the beginning of life, the spark, the birth, or idea for a project or organization. It is the concept. Anything is possible. Everything is new. There are no restraints.	**Aries in polarity: Aries-Libra**. Both signs are about beginnings and initiation. Aries is the initiation of the self, while Libra is the initiation into relationship and the world. Aries is the emergence of the being as an individual, Libra is the emergence of the being into the world of connections.

Taurus

Planetary Ruler: Venus
Element: Earth
Modality: Fixed

Body Part: Neck, shoulders
Season: Blooming bulbs
Archetype: The Bull

Mythology: The Search for Value & Meaning; the Minotaur; Moon Goddesses; Dionysus; Hephaestus

Taurus is the expression of hard work, of rootedness, of inner security, of certainty. It is the most dense sign and represents our connection to Earth. It is the work-horse sign and the sign which bears the brunt of all the excesses of the other signs. It is determined and immovable, perseverant and controlled. A planet in Taurus can anchor the chart and offer sustaining power and support for other planets. The planet in Taurus is loyal and trustworthy and will likely develop slowly over time. Taurus offers the native a sense of stability and a longing for security. The planet in Taurus will likely exhibit patience and an awareness of its surroundings and purpose.

What to stay aware of: A tendency of the planet in Taurus to stagnate, stubbornly stand in one place beyond the flow of life or to resist change, life and the possibility of an infinite universe.

Taurus responds to Aries by being cautious, caring and careful, considerate and grounded. Taurus thinks before acting and feels responsible. It is a sign of hard work, determination and tending to the land and the physical world. Taken to an extreme, Taurus feels the weight of the world, sinks its heels in stubbornly and gets stuck in the mud. Stagnation can be an issue.	**Taurus: Growth** In the second stage we grow as toddlers, focusing on the physical, the body. These are important years for care and nutrition. In an organization, we focus on resources, gathering money and collecting what we need to get off the ground. We hire staff, buy or rent a space and make the product.	**Taurus in polarity: Taurus-Scorpio** Both signs are about depth and intensity. Taurus digs in, while Scorpio moves out. Taurus grounds us while Scorpio strikes out.

Gemini

Planetary Ruler: Mercury
Element: Air
Modality: Mutable

Body Part: Arms, hands, lungs
Season: Flowery
Archetype: The Twins

Mythology: The Search for Variety; Castor and Pollux; Peter Pan; Hermes

Gemini is the sign that offers the planets an ability to search and find themselves. It is a sign which helps the planet find many opportunities, and many things to do and think. Gemini helps the planet to find possibility where others see none. Intellectual curiosity, open-mindedness and a disarming personality are other qualities that accompany this sign. Gemini expresses its abundance of mental energy and need for stimulation. The planet in Gemini loves to stay on the surface where it can keep moving with the greatest speed. This planet needs to experience itself in many different forms and ways. It is constantly searching for the spice of life—longing to see itself from many different perspectives.

Things to watch out for: The planet in Gemini may move in many directions at once without focus. It may seek variety at the expense of depth. It may alight quickly on a topic and leave considering itself an expert with a minimum of exposure.

| Gemini in response to Taurus offers endless possibilities, new ideas and abundant curiosity. It is a sign of exploring and thinking and communicating and looking at many sides of a situation. It is anything but stagnant. In extreme, Gemini is unfocused, unclear and scattered. | Gemini: Learning
Gemini represents early childhood, learning, exploring and communicating. In an organization, we open the doors. It is the stage where people are very busy doing things, multi-tasking and wearing many hats. Things are a little chaotic, but exciting with many possibilities. | Gemini in polarity: Gemini-Sagittarius
Both signs are about exploration, learning and communication. Gemini explores the inner realms, while Sagittarius explores the world. Gemini gathers information, while Sagittarius disseminates information. Gemini sees what is right in front, while Sagittarius sees the big picture. |
|---|---|---|

Cancer

Planetary Ruler: Moon
Element: Water
Modality: Cardinal

Body Part: Breast, womb
Season: Birth of summer
Archetype: The Crab

Mythology: The Search for Mother Goddess; Demeter; Kuan Yin

Cancer is the sign that takes us into the womb. We learn about safety, security, nurturing, and mothering. The emotions take a front and center role. We experience longings. We feel things. Concerns about intimacy are highlighted. Cancer asks us to look deeply into where we get our bread from, what our roots are, and who/what nurtures us. Often we must have tenacity and a strong inner life in order to deal with the energies of Cancer. Vulnerability, sensitivity and a tendency to attach significantly often accompany this cardinal water sign.

Things to watch out for: Becoming crabby when boundaries are crossed, being overly sensitive. The planet in Cancer may cling to a perception of security that keeps it too small.

Cancer grounds Gemini in the arena of connection and emotions. Cancer is a sign of intimacy and home. While a water sign, the Crab goes on land and water using its claws to grab onto earth. Cancer wants depth in relationship and focus on the hearth and love. It is the sign of the Mother and longs for security. Taken to an extreme, Cancer issues are feeling needy, insecure and overly emotional.	**Cancer: Adolescence** Exploring connection with others, intimacy and security. Learning about relationship — the focus of our teenage years. In an organization we focus on creating a foundation. We may need to step out of the stress of go-go and reorganize internally, paying attention to employee or self needs — caring for the emotional and physical well being of those involved.	**Cancer in polarity:** **Cancer-Capricorn** Both signs are about security. Cancer is about inner security in the feeling realm, while Capricorn is about outer security and the ability to make a living. Cancer is connected with emotional balance and stability while Capricorn is about stability in the world.

Leo

Planetary Ruler: Sun
Element: Fire
Modality: Fixed

Body Part: Heart
Season: Hot days of summer
Archetype: The Lion

Mythology: The Search for Being and Wholeness; Hercules; Rhea

The sign Leo colors planets with majesty, passion, royalty and self-confidence. There is power and egotism in this sign. Leo serves the function of helping us express ourselves clearly, strongly, and with perseverance. A sign of courage, direction, leadership, drive, love, and ambition. Leo may want to take over and rule while it also wants what is best for everyone.

What to be aware of: Planets in Leo can be overly focused on self and be overpowering. Leo is attributed to narcissism and being unaware of others' feelings.

| Leo the Lion responds with a loud roar of courage and inspiration. This fire sign is a sign of leadership, direction and strength. It emits a scent of power and aliveness that others just want to follow. Self-expression and creativity are also highlighted. Taken to an extreme, Leo can be arrogant, uncaring, overpowering and ruthless. | **Leo: Prime**
 The twenties, going forth into the world, charging full steam ahead. (Aren't we all a little arrogant in our twenties? I know I was.) The organization, having developed internally and reorganized is ready to meet the world head on and emerge fully and successfully. This is in our culture the prime of life and the prime of an organization. Vibrancy and health are highlighted. | **Leo in polarity:**
 Leo-Aquarius
 Both Leo and Aquarius are about expression and connection to the group. Leo must stand out in the group and needs to express itself as unique. Aquarius expresses itself through the group as one of, rather than separate from the group. Leo expresses itself more passionately, actively and artistically. Aquarius expression is creative in an intellectual, mental, innovative way. |

Virgo

Planetary Rulers: Chiron, Mercury
Element: Earth
Modality: Mutable

Body Part: Digestive organs
Season: The harvest
Archetype: The Virgin

Mythology: The Search for Meaningful Service, Virgin Mary

Planets in Virgo are asked to behave themselves, to serve other planets and to stay conscious. Virgo is the quality of clear, concise, attentive action. Often in life we are asked to "pay attention". When Virgo asks we must follow. Virgo is the "be here now" sign. In Virgo we possess the ability to stay focused, be careful and pay attention. Virgo challenges us to keep it simple, keep it clean and keep it clear. The planets in Virgo must operate through intense introspection, honest self-evaluation and perfect attendance.

What to be aware of: A tendency of planets in Virgo is to be overly concerned with being perfect, acting perfect or appearing perfect. Sometime planets in Virgo can be overly focused on the small stuff, the details and miss opportunities and the chance for expansion and vision.

Virgo responds to Leo by being humble, and by focusing on the moment and the details of ordinary living. Virgo is the sign of being human—everyday human life. It is the sign of the healer and caring for the body. Virgo gets things done, and can be very Zen—very in the moment. Clear, concise and clever. Taken to an extreme, Virgo can be overly particular, needing everything to be perfect and too demanding of itself and others.	**Virgo: The Work Years** The thirties, years when we are focused on making a living, creating a family, developing a career or path of service and attention to the daily aspects of living. An organization, having found its path of expression in Leo, sets to the task of maintaining that charge. Organization and tending to clarity and care in the work place are highlighted.	**Virgo in polarity: Virgo-Pisces** Both Virgo and Pisces care about service and spirituality. While Virgo is about being in the moment, being here and now, being in human form, Pisces is about being everywhere all at once, being in spirit, the oneness and connection of all. Both signs lead you to the same place through different expressions. Virgo is attentive to time and existence while Pisces is about transcending time and existence.

The Signs of the Zodiac

Libra

Planetary Ruler: Venus, Juno
Element: Air
Modality: Cardinal

Body Part: Kidneys
Season: Fall, wind, leaves falling
Archetype: The Scales

Mythology: The Search for the Soul Mate, Juno, Eros, Psyche

In Libra, the planet finds its path through mirroring, looking at the opposite or by going from one extreme or one side to another. There is constant juggling and the planet needs to interact with other planets. It is in that way that the planet in Libra finds its truest form of expression. In this way, Libra is the sign of relationship. When the Sun is in Libra it is fall in the Northern Hemisphere and we find ourselves going inward, preparing for winter and turning towards the necessities of life. The planets in Libra are looking for what is needed and are longing for connection.

What to watch out for: The planet in Libra may waffle in its effect while nothing is accomplished or experienced.

Libra is a sign of kindness, compassion, and being able to see both sides of a situation. It is the diplomat and responds to Virgo by offering a new way of seeing things that is filled with caring. Libra is focused on the other, the mirror and seeing the duality in life. Taken to an extreme, Libra can stay on the surface needing everything to stay calm and everyone to be happy along with indecisive and uncertain.	**Libra: Caring and Connection** The forties, focus on relationship with others, family or the world. Career paths are more settled and there is a focus on how to care for others and make a difference in the world. In an organization, success has been attained and the organization looks toward developing a connection with the rest of the world or at least that organization's sphere of influence. Developing a reputation and making a mark in the world are a focus.	**Libra in polarity: Libra-Aries** Both signs are about beginnings and initiation. Aries is the initiation of the self, while Libra is the initiation into relationship and the world. Aries is the emergence of the being as an individual; Libra is the emergence of the being into the world of connections. Aries sees itself alone and Libra sees itself in the mirror of the other.

Scorpio

Planetary Ruler: Pluto, Mars
Element: Water
Modality: Fixed

Body Part: Reproductive organs, colon
Season: Fall, dying time, dark time

Archetype: The Scorpion
Mythology: The Search for Transformation; Shakti; Persephone

In Scorpio the planet dives deep into its nature, longs to express itself powerfully without hesitation, and with intensity. The planet in Scorpio needs to be honest at the core. The planet asks to be transformed, challenged to do the right thing and fully empowered to act on its behalf. The planet in Scorpio requires that whatever it interacts with must be willing to look at itself deeply. There is no hesitation to speak or hold up the mirror of truth.

What to be aware of: The tendency of a planet in Scorpio to uncaringly reveal truth, to be secretive or to want to destroy what gets in its way.

Scorpio responds by taking us to the depths. It is a sign of truth at any cost, intensity and willingness to travel to the darkside or shadow to reclaim what is hidden from us. It is a sign of transformation, death to old, out-moded ways and power. Taken to an extreme, Scorpio can be manipulative using its power in unclear ways.	**Scorpio: Transformation** The fifties bring menopause, sexual transformation, looking deeply at the meaning of life, empty nest and often the aging and or loss of parents. In an organization, it brings a deeper looking at its purpose. Sometimes the organization begins to die if a deeper meaning is not found. Honesty and realness are emphasized.	**Scorpio in polarity: Scorpio-Taurus** Both signs are about depth and intensity. Taurus digs in, while Scorpio moves out. Taurus grounds us while Scorpio strikes out.

Sagittarius

Planetary Ruler: Jupiter
Element: Fire
Modality: Mutable

Body Part: Thighs
Season: Winter sleep and dreams

Archetype: The Archer
Mythology: The Search for Wisdom, Artemis, Athena

Sagittarius instills in the planet the longing for knowledge. The planet needs to search, explore, seek and find its true nature. There is hope and optimism in the journey and the Sagittarius quality of believing that there is an answer that can be found lights the way for this to be so. Planets in Sagittarius need lots of room, need lots of challenges and enjoy lots of social activity.

What to watch out for: The tendency of the planet in Sagittarius to be wearing rose-colored glasses and take off without notice or a clear plan and with a lack of boundaries.

| Sagittarius responds by taking the intensity of Scorpio and directing it toward knowledge and wisdom. With Sagittarius we are searching for the meaning of life, willing to take chances for opportunities, and believe that anything is possible. Sagittarius likes being in a group and being social. It can see the big picture. Taken to the extreme, Sagittarius can be out-to-lunch, unrealistic, extravagant and excessive. | **Sagittarius: Exploration** The sixties can bring retirement, travel, a new lease on life, seeking for new experiences. An organization, if it does not die at Scorpio, gives back to the world a vision of hope and prosperity. New things are possible. A rebirth can take place. | **Sagittarius in polarity: Gemini-Sagittarius** Both signs are about exploration, learning and communication. Gemini explores the inner realms, while Sagittarius explores the world. Gemini gathers information, while Sagittarius disseminates information. Gemini sees what is right in front; Sagittarius sees the big picture. |

The Signs of the Zodiac

Capricorn

Planetary Ruler: Saturn
Element: Earth
Modality: Cardinal

Body Part: Knees
Season: Winter
crystallization of forms

Archetype: The Sea-Goat, The Goat
Mythology: The Search for Life Path; Pan; Saturn; Father Time, Cronus

Capricorn is the sign that helps us to be on the planet, ground in reality and bring things into form. The planet in Capricorn longs for "reality", tends to be responsible for its own nature, tends to ground other planets and can set clear boundaries. This is the "no" sign, where a clear responsible no is often a yes to manifesting in another way. Capricorn is the sign of manifestation, bringing physical things into form and holding up its end of the bargain with integrity and perseverance. Planets in Capricorn are here to help move energy from the spirit realms into the physical, third-dimensional world.

What to be aware of: A planet in Capricorn—through an ability to be overly competent—may have high expectations, have a desire to control and have a tendency to say "no" before truly understanding what is needed or being asked of it.

Capricorn, the responsible sign, offers a more realistic and grounded perspective. Capricorn views the world through matter and the physical—everything is matter of fact and of course. Organized, competent and able to respond to any situation, Capricorn is the energy of success and ambition. Taken to an extreme, Capricorn can be controlling, dogmatic and skeptical.	**Capricorn: Crone years** The seventies can bring wisdom, accepting the responsibility of being an elder, acknowledging the reality of death. An organization takes on the responsibility of making a difference in the world, making a significant change.	**Capricorn in polarity: Cancer-Capricorn** Both signs are about security. Cancer is about inner security in the feeling realm, while Capricorn is about outer security and the ability to make a living. Cancer is connected with emotional balance and stability while Capricorn is about stability in the world.

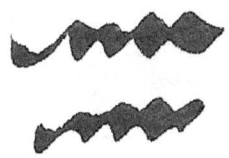

Aquarius

Planetary Ruler: Uranus
Element: Air
Modality: Fixed

Body Part: Ankles
Season: Preparing for Spring, waiting time

Archetype: The Water-bearer
Mythology: The Search for the Holy Grail, Prometheus, Pandora

Planets in Aquarius long for freedom, have a way of seeing the big picture, want life to change, enjoy change, and even thrive on change. The planets tend to exhibit intellectual gifts, an ability for invention, thinking outside the box and eccentricity of nature. The planet operates outside of the bounds of what is culturally considered "normal".

What to be aware of: The tendency for planets in Aquarius to be aloof—disconnected from reality, from emotions, from life, from their nature and truth.

Aquarius responds to Capricorn by thinking outside of the box, seeking freedom for all and equality. It is the sign of invention, high-minded thinking, creative intelligence and group consciousness. It is a sign of anarchy, throwing off the old and bringing in the new. Taken to the extreme, Aquarius can be rebellious without caring, and aloof emotionally—caring only for ideals and the cause at hand.	**Aquarius: Giving back** The eighties, gathering in group, friends, giving back wisdom, teaching, offering a new vision. An organization merges with other organizations or at least shares resources.	**Aquarius in polarity: Leo-Aquarius** Both Leo and Aquarius are about expression and connection to the group. Leo must stand out in the group and needs to express itself as unique. Aquarius expresses itself through the group as one of, rather than separate from the Aquarian group. Leo expresses itself more passionately, actively and artistically. Aquarius expression is creative in an intellectual, mental, innovative way.

Pisces

Planetary Rulers: Neptune, Jupiter
Element: Water
Modality: Mutable

Body Part: Feet
Season: The swelling of the seed in the earth

Archetype: The Fishes
Mythology: The Search for Peace; Christ; Percival

Planets in this the last of the signs are allowed to roam freely. They are cut loose and free to wander in search of their spiritual origins. The nature of a planet in Pisces is to give selflessly, love unconditionally and accept all that goes on in and around it. The planet loses itself in order to merge with something much larger. In the process the planet's nature is dissolved into the rest of the chart and expressed in relation to the whole of the experience of the individual.

What to be aware of: The tendency of the planet to prematurely transcend; in other words, the planet's energies may become lost to the individual before becoming wholly integrated into the experience and calling of the entire chart.

Pisces, the spiritual and all caring sign, responds to Aquarius' rebellion by offering a soothing perspective of love and kindness. Pisces is the sign that represents the interconnectedness of all life, all existence. It is Big love, Divinity, and diving into the ocean of the emotions. Feed the world and care for the sick. Taken to the extreme, Pisces can be unfocused, lacking in boundaries, spacey and lost.	**Pisces: Dissolving into Oneness** Merging with All That Is. Letting go of the body. Spirituality and meeting the Maker. The company no longer is a separate entity either by dissolving or merging.	**Pisces in polarity: Virgo-Pisces** Both Virgo and Pisces are about service and spirituality. While Virgo is about being in the moment, being here and now, being in human form, Pisces is about being everywhere all at once, being in spirit, the oneness and connection of all. Both signs lead you to the same place through different expressions. Virgo is attentive to time and existence while Pisces is about transcending time and existence.

Sign	Symbol	Archetype	Element	Quality	Ruler
Aries	♈	Ram	Fire	Cardinal	Mars
Taurus	♉	Bull	Earth	Fixed	Venus
Gemini	♊	Twins	Air	Mutable	Mercury
Cancer	♋	Crab	Water	Cardinal	Moon
Leo	♌	Lion	Fire	Fixed	Sun
Virgo	♍	Virgin	Earth	Mutable	Chiron (Mercury)
Libra	♎	Scales	Air	Cardinal	Venus
Scorpio	♏	Scorpion	Water	Fixed	Pluto (Mars)
Sagittarius	♐	Archer	Fire	Mutable	Jupiter
Capricorn	♑	Goat-fish	Earth	Cardinal	Saturn
Aquarius	♒	Water-bearer	Air	Fixed	Uranus
Pisces	♓	Fishes	Water	Mutable	Neptune

The Signs of the Zodiac

The Planets

The Planets are the main building blocks in the astrological chart. They represent the energies, the characters in the drama of our lives. They are the "what" in the chart. Each planet has its own expression and mythology. Where the planet is in the chart tells us how its energy manifests in our life.

If we think about the planets as blocking energy from the universe, then the planets are the facets of life that we are working with. They are the laws of the physical Universe. Each planet has a message for us. The message offers us a clue to greater wholeness. It is as if the planets are taking away that which we need to learn. While we are learning about all of the energies of the planets, the sign, house and aspects tell us the specific nature that was absent or less when we were born and that which we are thus filling or finding in our lives. Some planets may be in a more challenged position and some may be in an easier place and so we have more or less to learn about that particular Universal Law. Whether a planet is challenged or in flow is dependent on myriad factors including which aspects are involved, whether it is in a sign that is congenial to its energy and which house it is in.

Exercise: The Planets

Reflect on the following questions for your life. Write as much or a little as you like. Try doing this without thinking—just write whatever first comes into your mind.

1. Describe your essence.

2. Describe your emotional life.

3. Describe how you think and how you learn.

4. Describe your inner relationship with yourself.

5. Describe your assertiveness and drive.

6. Describe the prosperity and abundance in your life.

7. Describe your greatest lessons in life.

8. Describe your relationship to change.

9. Describe your spiritual journey.

10. Describe your understanding of death.

11. Describe your soul's calling.

The Planets

The Symbols

I look at the natal chart as a resonant system—a resonant system that includes waves of energy interacting at various angles. Symbols are used to express the energies where words fall short. Symbols are the embodiment of energies. The symbols in astrology are very powerful.

While the symbols for the signs are ancient glyphs based on the mythology of the Zodiac, the planetary symbols can be broken down into four main components.

o	=	*the circle is eternity, the never ending, spirit*
.	=	*a simple dot is pure potential and the emergence of power*
) or (	=	*a semi-circle is the soul, spirit reflected in a being*
+	=	*the material world, the finite, the cross of matter*

An entire interpretation of the planets can be realized from dissecting the planet symbols into these four components.

Become familiar with the following symbols either through repetitive writing or through drawing them or however you can. Looking at the components can help in order to remember the symbols. It is enormously helpful to have them memorized and in your cells.

Planet		
Sun	☉	Spirit encapsulates potential. The potential moves through spirit.
Moon	☽	The soul mirrors the soul. The spirit is split into the soul seeing the soul.
Mercury	☿	Soul moves through spirit into matter—the essence of communication.
Venus	♀	Matter upholds spirit—the essence of magnetism and attraction.
Mars	♂	Originally, a cross over a circle the opposite of Venus. Spirit is expressed through matter—moves through matter. The essence of the will force.
Jupiter	♃	The soul directs and inspires matter. The essence of growth.
Saturn	♄	Matter directs the soul. The soul moves into form. The essence of manifestation and incorporation.
Uranus	♅	The soul sees itself through matter as the spirit expresses itself through matter. The essence of change.
Neptune	♆	Matter penetrates the soul. Matter pierces the soul. Matter becomes aware of soul and soul becomes aware of matter. The essence of love.
Pluto	♇	The soul embraces the spirit and is upheld by matter. The essence of transformation.
Earth	⊕	The spirit encapsulates matter. The essence of the spirit of the world—of universal consciousness—of the fusion of matter and spirit.

The Sun

Universal Law:
The observer cannot observe without altering what is observed.

The Sun in a natal chart shows us where our greatest vitality and individual essence lies. It is our light into and out of this world. It is our unique radiance. To honor the qualities of our Sun sign is to support our own unique essence. To allow the light into our lives is to accept the conditions of our Sun—its placement, aspects, rulership, sign and house. When we support our Sun we feel more alive, have more energy and have a brighter outlook on life. Our very nature alters that which is around us. Once our light is shone on a situation, we have changed it. The strength of our light and the quality of our essence determines how the world around us is affected. If we accept our Sun placement, we shine brighter and the world shines back for us. Our path becomes well lit and we have more sunny days on the journey.

What the Sun likes: Radiance, joy, self-expression, happiness

What the Sun dislikes: Negativity, dullness, energy drains

General Associations: Our vitality, our essence, who we know ourselves to be, courage, will to live, inner and outer strength, how we shine, how we feel alive, what lights us up, our true identity, our ego, self-esteem, our radiance

Rules: Leo   Detriment: Aquarius   Exaltation: Aries   Fall: Libra

Cycle: 365 1/4 days

Astronomical: approximately 1,000,000 miles in diameter, about 93 million miles from Earth, takes 25.45 Earth-days to rotate on its axis, takes 225 million Earth-years to revolve around the Milky Way

Medical Rulerships: Heart and circulatory system, vital forces, circulation of the blood, well-being of the spinal cord, physical growth in general, energy, prana, he constitutional quality of the body, inflammation, infection, fever, energy problems, heart disorder, cell vitality

Vitamins: Vitamin D and C
Herbs: Borage, Hawthorn
Foods: Fruits and vegetables, fish
Color: Yellow
Gems: Ruby, cat's eye, garnet, tiger's eye, corundum
Note: B-flat

Aromas: Melissa, Benzoin, Neroli, Patchouli, Orange, Grapefruit
Metal: Gold
Tarot Card: The Sun
Occupations: Royalty, brokers, bankers, government officials, CEOs, self-employment, actors, leaders
Day of the Week: Sunday

Myths: Any hero or heroine myth is a solar myth. Our story books are full of them. King Arthur, Joan of Arc, Apollo, Luke Skywalker, Hercules, Samson, Indiana Jones, and if I dared to put Jesus in a category, I would put him here. We are a culture that worships the Sun, the glorious male principle of the Self. We elected a Solar hero out of the Sun Capital, the myth makers of our culture—Ronald Reagan, the actor from Hollywood—a hero actor no less. Egypt, a Sun-worshipping culture, had many solar gods and is a good culture to look to for information about Sun mythology.

In charts: This is the true self, who we are in our most vital sense of being. Where our Sun resides is the area we must honor in order to maintain a life force. Our sun sign is the sign we must accept, resonate with, honor, and know in order to experience life. It is one of, if not the most important points in the chart. Without attention to our Sun placement, we lose life energy, wither and ultimately die. (Since we all die anyway, I can say that.)

By transit: The Sun transits a place in a chart for only a day or two, hardly enough time to notice its effects. Since it never moves retrograde we do not get to feel the effect of it stationing. On Sun transit days, we can feel more alive, have more energy and have more focus for the area that is being transited. A Sun transit may set off a more long-term transit. This usually happens in pleasant ways, in ways that open us to a greater potential within ourselves.

Exercise: The Sun

To learn about your Sun: Do something that invigorates you.

If your Sun is in:	Do:	How:
Aries	go on an adventure, take a risk, tell someone you love them, spend time alone	spontaneously
Taurus	take a hike through dense forest, walk barefoot, dig in the dirt, plant something, paint or sculpt, do a craft, spend time in nature	slowly and savoring every minute of it
Gemini	meet someone new, journal, talk to a friend, read a book about something you know nothing about, spend time with your neighbor or a sibling	while other events are going on
Cancer	redecorate your space, bake something, take a bath or do something nurturing, spend time with mom	sensitively, with care
Leo	sing, dance, act, perform, exercise (only if it's fun), play a game, give a speech, spend time with children	passionately, playfully
Virgo	take your vitamins, clean your space, clear your clutter, do yoga, organize your drawers, spend time with an animal	meticulously
Libra	do something outside with someone else, spend time with a partner or loved one	peacefully, harmoniously
Scorpio	bring up a topic that has been considered taboo, explore caves, go deep sea diving, spend time with grandparents, find out about your ancestry	intensely, honestly
Sagittarius	take a road trip, learn something new, read philosophy, create a celebration or just go to one, spend time with anyone you meet in your travels	outrageously, do it big
Capricorn	plan your next career move, set an intention for something you wish to change about your life, re-organize your systems, spend time with a co-worker	certainly, with integrity and confidently
Aquarius	gather a group of friends together for a specific purpose, write a letter to the editor, visit a museum, spend time with friends	Innovatively, eccentrically
Pisces	write poetry, meditate, pray, go on a retreat, be near water, pay attention to your dreams, spend time alone	mystically, peacefully, alone

The Moon

Universal Law:
What we feel, we can heal. The power of the emotions to direct energy.

The Moon is the emotional body in the chart. We interact with life through our moon. We process situations, conversations and any stimulus through our Moon body. We allow experiences to happen according to our receptivity to life. How able we are to allow life in, to receive from the Universe, to accept the conditions we have been given—this is seen in the Moon in the chart. The Moon tells us how we naturally feel nurtured, feel loved, feel welcomed, feel warmth. The placement of the Moon tells us how we let life touch us—our emotional intelligence and our general acceptance of life.

What the Moon likes: Feelings, emotions
What the Moon dislikes: Control issues
General Associations: Feelings, emotional life, receptive side, how we feel nurtured, how our vitality is reflected or seen, mother, unconscious, our longings, what is reflected back to us from the world

Rules: Cancer   Detriment: Capricorn   Exaltation: Taurus   Fall: Scorpio

Cycle: 28 days

Astronomical: Orbits around the Earth in 28 and a 1/4 days, simultaneously spins so that we only ever see one side of it, 2,160 miles in diameter.

Medical Rulerships: Mucous membranes, stomach, bladder, ovaries, uterus, breasts, stomach, tear ducts, sympathetic nervous system, lymphatics, menstruation, flow of bodily secretions, conditions of health, fluids in the body, allergic reactions, emotional disorder, bodily secretions, mucus formation, altered body rhythms, acute ailments

Vitamins: none
Herbs: Mugwort, hops
Foods: Dairy products, tofu
Colors: Silver, white, pale blue, opalescent and iridescent colors
Gems: Opal, moonstone, pearl
Note: A-flat

Aromas: Cypress, juniper
Metal: Silver
Tarot Card: The Priestess

Occupations: Counselor, mother, anything that nurtures others, midwives, nurses, fishermen, seamen, longshoremen, restaurant servers

Day of the Week: Monday

Myths: Kuan Yin, Selena, Mary Mother of Christ, Jemaya, Isis, Diana. All Mother myths are moon myths, particularly Demeter.

In charts: The Moon is our emotional life, our feelings, and our receptive nature. It is our conditioning. It represents our mother or the more nurturing parent. It represents our home and how we feel at home in the world. It is what we need—what we need to feel nurtured, to feel whole, to feel comforted. We must pay attention to our moon placement in order to feel safe and nurtured in this world. The moon rules phases and moods. The moon placement is an indication of how we receive input, information and how we process what is shown to us and given to us.

By transit: The Moon moves so fast that it aspects a planet in our chart for a mere several hours. However, watching the phases of the Moon and the Moon signs are excellent ways to tune into the nature of the day and time. The Moon can trigger an event stirred by a longer-term transit—especially eclipses and full and new Moons. The Moon joining our natal Moon is called a lunar return and is symbolic of the beginning of our own personal month.

Exercise: The Moon

To learn about your Moon: Do something nurturing. Cook a delicious meal. Take a bath. Get a massage. Care for yourself in some way.

If your Moon is in:	In order to get in touch with feelings and feel nurtured:	How:
Aries	take a risk to tell someone how you feel about them	spontaneously
Taurus	paint or do some form of art, spend time in nature, get a massage, touch someone, get dirty	slowly and savoring every minute of it
Gemini	get together with a friend and talk until you can't talk anymore, write in your journal	while other events are going on
Cancer	since the tears come easily anyway, just allow yourself the time and space to feel them, hug someone	sensitively, with care
Leo	do something physically challenging and/or invigorating	passionately, playfully
Virgo	clean, clear and spend time with a pet	meticulously
Libra	go on a date or spend time processing your current relationship	peacefully, harmoniously
Scorpio	dance, do ritual, express yourself sexually, look deeply at an issue with the help of another	intensely, honestly
Sagittarius	read a spiritual book or a philosophical book, seek to understand something new about your own nature	outrageously, do it big
Capricorn	speak the truth, set an intention, set aside a certain amount of time to think about your life and goals, consider your life	certainly, with integrity and confidently
Aquarius	do something you have never done before, get together with friends, (feelings? what feelings? – don't worry, they are in there)	Innovatively, eccentrically
Pisces	do something alone near water, take a spiritual retreat, get away from others so that your feelings are really your own	mystically, peacefully, alone

Mercury

Universal Law:
Intention is the creation of matter. Our thoughts create our reality.

Mercury in the natal chart tells us about the nature of our thinking process—how our mind works, how we learn and process information. The Moon tells us how we receive the information—Mercury tells us how we interpret that information once it is received. An examination of Mercury in the chart will tell us how we communicate—how the words come out of our mouth. Mercury is the messenger and it relays to us what is going on. Mercury shows us how we analyze input and distribute output. Our intentions come from Mercury—our declarations to the world. Mercury is ambidextrous and a hermaphrodite—neutral in many ways. Mercury does not carry emotion, pain or sensitivity. It is merely the way our mental body processes information. Mercury loves to travel and think and do puzzles and talk about the weather. He does not long for depth or honesty—only that something is said. Mercury expects us to talk to each other, write to each other and solve problems.

What Mercury likes: Talking, writing, communication, magic

What Mercury does not like: Bickering, dishonesty, power plays, withholding information

General Associations: Spoken and written communication, messenger, how we think, our thought processes, the mind, how we learn, mental, intellect, connection, active intelligence, reasoning facilities, inventive abilities, ability to learn language, progress through experimentation, restlessness, versatility, dexterity, inconsistency, superficiality

Rules: Gemini, Virgo   Detriment: Sagittarius, Pisces   Exaltation: Aquarius   Fall: Leo

Cycle: Yearly orbit is 87.97 Earth days; moves retrograde 3 times each year for approximately 3 weeks, one day on Mercury is equal to 58.65 Earth-days, so in 2 years on Mercury there are exactly 3 days, axis tilt is 0 degrees

Astronomical: Average diameter is only 2900 miles—not much bigger than our moon's; 760° F average temperature

Medical Rulerships: Respiratory system, central nervous system, hands, tongue, thyroid gland, vocal cords, bronchial tubes, lungs, hearing, sight, respiration, reflexes, functions of the nerves, mental attitudes, all tubing in the body, mental disorders, respiratory disorders, nervous disorders, hormonal imbalance, speech

Vitamins: B complex
Herbs: Nervine herbs, catnip, skullcap
Foods: Whole grains
Colors: Metallic shades of blue, plaids and checks
Gems: Emerald, peridot, agates, apatite, apophyllite, tiger's eye
Note: F-sharp and C
Aromas: Cardamom, hyssop, fennel, lavender, rosemary, thyme, peppermint
Metal: Quicksilver, glass, gold
Tarot Card: The Magician
Lower Octave of Uranus: Mercury is about Lower Mind — human mind; Uranus is about Higher Mind
Occupations: Orators, writers, educators, librarians, postal workers, accountants, engineers, statisticians, secretaries
Day of the Week: Wednesday
Myth: Mercury is the God of Wisdom. He is the trickster and the magician. In Egypt he is Thoth. In Greece he is Hermes. In India he is Saram, the divine watchman who watches the stars

In charts: Mercury tells us how our minds work. In earth signs the mind will work slower but with greater attention, determination and retention. In air signs the mind works swiftly, easily and with great flexibility and agility while often being restless and easily distracted. In water signs the mental processes contain an emotional component — the person feels their thoughts — they tend to learn more kinesthetically. In fire, Mercury has many ideas, learns quickly and can initiate new concepts while often lacking in retention and memory.

By transit: Mercury transits planets in our natal charts so quickly that the effects are often not noticeable. (It typically takes only a day for Mercury to transit a natal planet.) If we do notice the effects they are of a mental nature where we may be more mentally stimulated or less depending on what is being transited and if any other planets are involved. Mercury by transit more often acts as a trigger planet. When Mercury conjuncts or opposes the point of a longer lasting transit, it may send into motion events of the nature of the longer lasting transit. Most importantly, when Mercury goes retrograde, the effects of its transit are more noticeable. Mercury can offer more alertness when moving directly. During Mercury retrograde, Mercury calls us to go within, be more contemplative, quiet and reflective.

Exercise: Mercury

Mercury is in:	Honor your Mercury:	How:
Aries	Say the thing that no one else is willing to say — at least dare yourself to think the thing that no one else is talking about; take five minutes to write without taking your pen off the paper without censoring what you are writing	spontaneously
Taurus	Try calligraphy or using special pens and then write something not because you have anything to say — but because writing is beautiful	slowly and savoring every minute of it
Gemini	Read a magazine, newspaper or short story to get inspired — or a book with little known facts, then write a non-fictional piece about what you just read. Mercury in Gemini is an excellent sign for writing and for speaking (sometimes non stop) — so get tuned into your audience. Who are you writing for?	while other events are going on
Cancer	Your thinking and writing needs to be accessed through the emotions — so whatever you say or write you need to feel first. Pick something to communicate about that has meaning for you.	sensitively, with care
Leo	This is an excellent sign for oration and public speaking — so join toastmasters or get out there with your thoughts and opinions.	passionately, playfully
Virgo	Another good sign for the pen on paper form of communication. Non-fiction, requiring meticulous research is a particular talent — so give it a try.	meticulously
Libra	Write a letter to a friend or lover. Communicate or call someone that is close to you. Mediation and being able to assist others with disputes is an excellent exercise for you Mercury in Libras.	peacefully, harmoniously
Scorpio	Truth telling — no matter what. Since you tend to psychically pick up the thoughts of those around you and then need to send those thoughts away — take time to journal or write a passionate letter releasing the thoughts of others. Take time to research in depth a particular topic you have passion for.	intensely, honestly
Sagittarius	Read and travel to learn new things. Read non-fiction philosophical works. Read works from other cultures and then write an article to be published.	outrageously, do it big
Capricorn	Write a one-year, a five-year and a ten-year plan. Organize your thoughts and dreams on paper and prepare to present them to a group. Speech writing and using language to manage and organize projects is a particular skill you tend to have.	certainly, with integrity and confidently
Aquarius	Get together a group of folks and brainstorm. Have a simple intention to begin with and then get creative and out of the box.	Innovatively, eccentrically
Pisces	Write, read and listen to poetry. Get inspired by fiction and fantasy writing. Write your own fictional short story or novel.	mystically, peacefully, alone

Venus

Universal Law:
You attract to yourself who you are.
Manifestation occurs when what you desire aligns with your true feelings and your intention.

Venus invites us to tap into our longing. She tells us that we can have whatever we want as long as we can feel it in our hearts. She whispers sensuously to us that the Universe is ours for the taking. Nothing need get in our way if only we feel we deserve. And, indeed, Venus tells us that we do deserve what we want. Venus invites us to breathe deeply the beauty of this world—to enjoy its lusciousness, its abundance. Venus takes us to the feast of life—where there is plenty—plenty of love, art, yummy food and texture. Venus wants us to experience pleasure and earthy sensuality. Venus reminds us that we are in a body for a reason—that world is ours for the taking. Venus teaches us to enjoy being in a body—enjoy the sensations of falling in love, good sex, a long decadent meal, a Beethoven symphony, a Botticelli, a long walk in Paris.

What Venus likes: Love, art, sensuality, creativity, beauty

What Venus dislikes: Confrontation, dullness, dryness, boredom

General Associations: Art, love, what we attract to ourselves, receptivity, beauty, relationships, sensuality, appreciation of nature, sculpture, the ability of the individual to prosper in the material sense; spending and saving money and resources; personal magnetism; harmony, devotion, responsiveness

Rules: Taurus, Libra   Detriment: Scorpio, Aries   Exaltation: Pisces   Fall: Virgo

Cycle: 225 days; goes retrograde several times per year

Astronomical: brightest object in the sky after the Sun and Moon; diameter is 98% of Earth's, volume is 92% of Earth's, mass is 83% of Earth's; rotates backwards (from East to West) -the Sun rises in the West and sets in the East; a Venus day=243 Earth days, a Venus year= 224.7 Earth days, which means that a day on Venus is longer than a year on Venus; so on Venus every 27 days are equal to 25 years exactly; a great mantle of clouds veil her; surface temp=500° F; no moons

Medical Rulerships: Throat, thyroid gland; hair, skin, complexion, facial features, kidneys, thymus gland, venous circulation of the blood, reproductive system, beauty, what one likes in food; imbalance of bodily energies, benign growths, blood sugar imbalance, lack of tone, muscular or otherwise; illness that comes from excess; illness within the bladder

Minerals: Iodine, copper
Herbs: Dandelion leaf, uva ursi, alfalfa, licorice, anise
Foods: Sea vegetables, fish
Colors: Green, pink, pastel shades
Note: D
Gems: Diamond, jade, malachite, rose quartz, zircon, white coral
Aromas: Clary sage, myrrh, frankincense
Metal: Copper, brass, gold, platinum

Tarot Card: The Empress
Lower Octave of Neptune: Venus is about Human Love; Neptune is about Divine Love.
Occupations: Anything to do with the arts and music, beauticians, clothing and jewelry designers, botanists, florists, poets,
Day of the Week: Friday

Myth: When Saturn castrated his father, Uranus, he threw the testicles into the sea and Venus was born out of the foam of the sea. She married Vulcan the silversmith who was reported to be very ugly. She had many lovers, notably Mars and Mercury. To the Greeks, she is Aphrodite. To the Hindus, she is Lakshmi.

In the birth chart: Venus governs the laws of magnetism. Venus represents the ability to attract to ourselves that which we desire (Mars) and assimilate those things or people into our lifestyle. Venus rules the power of attraction, charisma and connection. It is a planet of relationship in that wherever Venus resides we are always relating to the world around us. Venus shows us how we see, feel, experience and appreciate beauty. Venus show us how we relate to ourselves and to each other. It is the planet of desiring connection, affection and love and how we go about getting it. Venus stirs our inner fires so that we can set outer fires through drawing to us that which we desire. Naturally, our desires do not always lead us down an easy, healthy or nurturing path. When we feel like we are always attracting the wrong people, the wrong situations, the wrong things to ourselves, we can look at Venus in the natal chart for greater understanding.

By Transit: The effects of Venus by transit are fairly minimal. It usually only transits a natal planet for one or two days. During these days, there is more energy for passion, artistic inspiration, cooking, crafts and acts of love. Transits of Venus are usually harmonious days, days good for buying art, for focus on beauty, i.e. getting your hair cut, facials and buying new clothes. Depending on the planet that it is transiting, watch for overindulgence.

The most significant Venus transits are when Venus is conjunct another planet or planets while it is transiting or if it is stationary moving direct or stationary moving retrograde. During stationary times, which can last up to three days, Venus has more opportunity to work her love magic and these times can signify a new relationship or love affair. In general, Venus transits are too short to indicate the beginning of a romance but under a stationary Venus, her powers multiply.

Exercise: Venus

To learn about your Venus: Do something creative. Make a collage. Paint. Draw. Sculpt. Create beauty. Get a facial or even a makeover. Buy a new outfit in which you feel stunning and radiant.

If your Venus is in:	Do:
Aries	Free flow movement
Taurus	Paint, play with clay, garden
Gemini	Free flow writing
Cancer	Redecorate your space, cook
Leo	Dance, sing, move
Virgo	Create beauty through simplicity
Libra	Make a collage, make music with others
Scorpio	Make love, create an art performance
Sagittarius	Visit an art gallery, museum, go to a concert
Capricorn	Do something crafty
Aquarius	Create a new outfit out of wild and eccentric clothes
Pisces	Write poetry, read poetry, take pictures

Mars

Universal Law:
If you want something in life, your free will has the power to go out and get it. You can do anything you want to do if you have the drive and the courage to go for it.

Mars wants us to take action in life. He wants us to get off the couch and make something happen. He does not care what it is, nor care what the consequences of our actions are. Mars just wants something to happen. Mars rules our will force. Mars says that we can do anything we want to do. Mars is a driving force. Mars tells us that all it takes is our own will force. Mars wants to hear nothing about fate. For Mars it's all free will. If we are determined and focused we can accomplish anything. Mars is the part of the decision making process that says "Yes, I'm going to do it" and then sets out to do it. Mars rules our actions in life—the things that we do. In a chart it tells us about our force field—how much energy we have to get stuff done—to make things happen. Mars has no patience for waiting and allowing things to happen. In our charts, the position of Mars tells us how to get things done, how determined we are and how much force we have to make life happen. Mars tells us how and to what degree our will operates.

What Mars likes: Action, assertiveness, courage, guts, drive, ambition

What Mars dislikes: Fear, weakness

General Associations: How we act, behavior, assertiveness, aggression, action, yang energy, desire, what we go out and get, decisiveness, wars, sports, competitiveness, the desire to be alive and human

Rules: Aries, Scorpio   Detriment: Libra, Taurus   Exaltation: Capricorn   Fall: Cancer

Cycle: 687 Earth Days; 24 1/2 hours to complete a rotation; has four distinct seasons; takes about 1 1/3 years to orbit the Earth

Astronomical: Diameter is 4,200 miles; has two small moons; the red planet; reaches as high as 80°F in the summer but even then drops far below 0°F in the evening

Medical Rulerships: Muscles, adrenal glands, blood, red corpuscles of the blood, the external reproductive organs, the excretory organs, muscle tissues, energy levels, get-up-and-go, how active we are, inflammation, rapid temperature increases, acids, infection, acute disease, fever, eruptive action, bruises, wounds, burns, irritation, ulcers, flare-ups, hemorrhages; fever, cuts, surgery; when Mars is retrograde — the system's ability to deploy energy and will is debilitated and susceptibility to illness is heightened

Vitamins: Iron

Herbs: Stinging nettles, yellow dock root, burdock root, cayenne

Foods: Dulse, liver, beets, blackstrap molasses, wheatgrass juice

Colors: Scarlet, red, magenta, claret, drab shades of brown and green

Note: D-flat

Gems: Red coral, carnelian, garnet, bloodstone, ruby

Aromas: Basil, black pepper, cinnamon, ginger

Metal: Iron, steel, silver, copper

Tarot Card: The Tower

Lower Octave of Pluto: Mars is about human desire; Pluto is about the desire of humanity to evolve.

Occupations: Military, metallurgists, surgeons, dentists, butchers, barbers, carpenters, trial lawyers

Day of the Week: Tuesday

Myth: The God of War. To the Greeks, Ares. To the Egyptians, Artes which gave us the word "arts" and points to the creative expression of Mars. To the Hindus, Mangala or Lohita or Kartikkeya.

In charts: Mars indicates how we behave, our inclination to take action and our ability to be powerful. Through the planet Mars we discover our strength, our will to live and our desire to improve our lives. Our drive for success, for sex and for power is found in the sign and house of Mars. With Mars, we instigate movement in our life. It is the planet that, along with Venus, helps move in and out of relationships.

In Fire signs, Mars acts with the greatest of ease — it can take action directly without vacillation or premeditation. Mars in Air signs can point to more erratic action or vacillation before action — a tendency to think first. Mars in Water indicates an emotional component to actions. Mars in Earth signs can indicate a thorough and slow ability to act.

By Transit: Mars, like Venus and Mercury, transits natal planets quickly — within two days. It may offer us an ability to take action, to be successfully assertive or it may stimulate a flare-up of anger or confrontation. A stationary Mars is a very powerful phenomenon to be aware of. We often feel a little more volatile, a little more heated and agitated during these times. We are called to action. If we hesitate we may feel frustrated. Retrograde Mars indicates a time to withdraw and turn our energy toward housecleaning, taking care of internal business and looking at our most intimate relationships.

Exercise: Mars

To learn about your Mars: Assert yourself in some way. Take action in your life where you have been resisting or avoiding.

Mars is in:	Do:
Aries	Take yourself outside and do something that gets your heart rate up. Dance. Play. Run around. Get into a competitive sport for the fun of it.
Taurus	Participate in a ground-breaking event. Go for a long walk in nature. Do yoga and hold a posture for a long time. Give yourself permission to slow down.
Gemini	Pick up a drum or any other instrument and play 'til any frustration or confusion is lifted. Pick up a hobby that supports focus — a hobby that completely transfixes you.
Cancer	Use movement to express your feelings. Any body-oriented therapy can be helpful to unleash the emotions. Massage and touch can also be very supportive.
Leo	Get outside and play in nature. Take a really long hike or get into backpacking. Get in touch with your voice and learn how to express yourself through clear speech.
Virgo	Take time to get yourself organized and clear. Make lists if needed. Give yourself permission to move things around in your work environment for increased clarity.
Libra	Find a way to have balance in your life. Justice and harmony are important to you so look at your life and see where you are out of balance. Ask for support to rebalance.
Scorpio	Dance, sing and move your body to a new rhythm. Take care of your physical body and get near water if you experience any toxicity in your body or emotions.
Sagittarius	Take a trip — even if just a day trip. Go someplace new — some place you have not been before. Take some time for study and reading.
Capricorn	Get organized. Make a plan and set deadlines for yourself. This a sign that has great fortitude for achieving goals once clarity about the goal is reached.
Aquarius	Go out on a limb to explore something that you consider wildly eccentric. Go out of bounds. Get out into wilderness.
Pisces	Follow your intuition without reservation. Take time to ask for a sign, for understanding and for knowing. Follow what is presented without trying to figure it out.

Jupiter

Universal Law:
Anything and everything is possible.

To honor Jupiter is to get rid of all obstacles. To allow Jupiter in your life is to accept that we live in an abundant loving Universe where anything can happen at any moment. We could win the lottery. We could fall in love. We could find God. We could get enlightened. Today. Jupiter says it is all about what you believe. If you believe it can happen, then it can. If you have Faith, then you can be healed, saved, loved, and have whatever you want. Jupiter is the good father, the sugar daddy and he is in charge. You need something, you can just pray to Jupiter and he will make it happen — if you believe.

What Jupiter likes: Joy, creative self-expression, abundant thinking, excess, expansion, growth

What Jupiter dislikes: Containment, restrictions, contracting out of fear, controlling behavior

General Associations: expansion, growth, gifts, abundance, largeness, where all things are possible

Rules: Sagittarius, Pisces   Detriment: Gemini, Virgo   Exaltation: Cancer   Fall: Capricorn

Cycle: 11-12 years

Astronomical: 88,700 miles in diameter; a day is only 10 Earth hours; -200° F

Medical Rulerships: Liver, pancreas, hip joints, thighs, intestines, blood plasma, posterior pituitary gland, cell nutrition, development of the formation of hemoglobin, expansion, lack of control, overeating, swelling, liver, fats of the body, enlarged organs, excess, fats, obesity, preserves life

Vitamins: Silica
Herbs: Dandelion root; chicory
Foods: Green leafy vegetables, sea vegetables
Colors: Blue-green, deep purple, deep blue
Note: F
Gems: Yellow sapphire, turquoise, topaz, citrine
Aromas: Cedarwood, Melissa, Sandalwood
Metal: Tin, gold
Tarot Card: Fortune
Occupations: Politics, judges, religion, higher education, philosophers, lawyers, explorers, travellers, philanthropists, fund-raisers
Day of the Week: Thursday

Myth: Zeus to the Greeks. The God of the Heavens. Ammon to the Egyptians. To the Hindus, Vishnu the Preserver. Jupiter divided the Universe into the Heavens, the Underworld and the Seas and gave the Underworld and the Seas to his brothers. He is the God that the other Gods and Goddesses came to for boons, gifts and help. He was almost always willing to help but often wound up getting something out of it for himself. He was known for having affairs with many of the Goddesses.

In charts: This is the place of expansion, our growing edge where we are always looking and searching. Jupiter points to where and how we believe that anything is possible. It is an area of talents and gifts. It points to where we are looking for the silver lining.

By transit: Jupiter opens us up to new possibilities. It shows that more is possible. We must grow, must open up. We can no longer accept the status quo, what is normal or what is expected of us. We want more. Jennifer Shafer, a fellow astrologer, calls Jupiter "the secret break-up agent" since when it transits a house or planet of relationship we often want something better, something bigger.

The twelve-year cycle is the Jupiter cycle and an important one to pay attention to. We may begin something new, open up to a new career, start school or begin a new relationship during a Jupiter transit. We may also experience important lessons for our growth not always as blissful as traditional Jupiter followers may lead you to believe.

Exercise: Jupiter

To learn about your Jupiter: Expand your life in some way. Open a door that you have been afraid to open. Believe that anything is possible and go for it.

If your Jupiter is in:	Do:
Aries	Go on an adventure. Take a few days off and drive somewhere without knowing where you are going. Take a trip without planning any of it.
Taurus	Look at what needs finishing in your life. Look at what needs nurturance. Take a look at what sustains your life and make a commitment to grow it, expand it and follow through with what needs tending.
Gemini	Study something new. Go to a library and randomly pick up a new book. Begin the study of something you are interested in for no good reason.
Cancer	Observe your family and home life. Who is your family and are you feeling nurtured by them? Do you like your home? Are there changes you would like to make to your home or family in order to feel that you are growing personally and in happiness.
Leo	Express yourself in some creative way. Get the word out about what you know and have to share with others. Take a risk to explore your voice and speech. Be willing to stand up for what you know in your cells is true for you.
Virgo	Take a good hard look at your work and determine how it is serving yourself and others. Is it challenging and rewarding? Ask yourself the hard questions and answer truthfully and then be willing to make changes if your answers are not satisfactory to yourself.
Libra	Take a trip with a close friend or lover. Explore the world of relationship or in relationship. Take a chance to express love and kindness.
Scorpio	Explore the nature of death and dying. What if you died today? Would you consider your life a "success" on your own terms? Take a deep look at how you are living so that death is not scary or inconvenient.
Sagittarius	At least once in your life, go on a major pilgrimage to a site that is sacred to you. In the meantime, take many smaller pilgrimages. Take time to study the classics or other philosophical and spiritual material.
Capricorn	Take a survey of your life and ask yourself if you have what you need. What does growth mean to you and how do you plan to expand your life to reach and affect more people with your goodness and clarity.
Aquarius	Gather a group of like-minded souls together and create a grass roots movement for change. Maybe start by joining a group that is already in existence that is doing what you believe in.
Pisces	Go on a retreat. Take some time away from the world to think your own thoughts and journey in your own imagination.

Saturn

Universal Law:
The law of karma – what you sow, you reap – to every action there is an equal and opposite reaction.

Saturn tells us there are consequences. He shows us where the lines are and what is safe and unsafe. Saturn shows us the reality of life. Saturn, in a way, rules all laws of the physical universe. You need to have a body to make certain things happen. If a wall is five feet away it will likely stay five feet away unless energy is enacted upon it to move it. Saturn tells that everything we do has an effect in the world. Every action has a reaction. Saturn holds us accountable for our actions. Saturn teaches us to be in integrity. Saturn demands honesty and accountability. Saturn expects us to be responsible, clear and direct. And above all, we must remember Karma. Everything we do has consequences and we must accept responsibility for the consequences of our actions and non-actions. Saturn does not let us get away with anything. Saturn is the father that protects us and teaches us responsibility. Saturn holds space for us while we learn and still allows us to feel our pain. Saturn lets us fall off the bike so we know how much it hurts or does not hurt. Saturn reminds us that there are ditches on the side of the road and sometimes he allows us drive into them. Sometimes, Saturn blocks all movement if we head toward one. Saturn in a chart tells us the area of life where we must be in integrity, where we must honor the reality of our life circumstances. Saturn in the chart also tells us how we are writing our life script. Saturn tells us that we are in control of our own lives – that no one else can tell us how to live our lives. Others may limit our options (according to Saturn), but no one else tells us how to live in our given circumstances. Saturn expects us to accept reality and get on with living our truest, most authentic expression.

What Saturn likes: Responsibility, clarity, honesty, integrity

What Saturn dislikes: Irresponsibility, recklessness, impulsiveness, unkindness, lies, weakness

The Planets – Saturn

The Law of Conservation of Energy — energy can be neither created nor destroyed. We can use energy to create new forms and Saturn is all about the creation of form. Saturn is our belief system that creates the limitations that we experience as "reality". Saturn represents the things that appear to get in the way. The lessons of Saturn show us that all life is an illusion, yet even then, we must acknowledge the laws of karma.

General Associations: Contraction, contracts, lessons, bringing intent into form, limitations, boundaries, constrictions, physical reality, constructs, belief systems, systems in general, authority, what the world wants from us, career and life path, karma

Rules: Capricorn   Detriment: Cancer   Exaltation: Aquarius   Fall: Leo

Cycle: Takes approximately 2 1/2 years to move through a sign, 29 years to move through the entire zodiac

Astronomical: Ten moons, rings circle around Saturn in the exact plane of Saturn's equator, a gaseous planet, density is the lowest of all the planets, length of Saturn day=10 1/2 Earth hours (spins very fast)

Medical Rulerships: The skeletal system, teeth, bones, joints, skin, gall bladder, ligaments, knees, calf, spleen, organs of hearing, ossification, congestion, functioning of the tendons and cartilage, hypo-functioning (sluggish), the frame of anything, chronic disease, hardening, cold, retention, calcification, obstruction, malignancy, stagnation; Parathyroid — controls the calcium metabolism; colds, constrictions, debilitation, and the chronic dimensions of illness

Vitamins/Minerals: Calcium
Herbs: Hemlock, rue, senna, comfrey, hemp, wintergreen
Color: Gray, black
Note: G

Gems: Blue sapphire, lapis lazuli, calcite, onyx, jet
Aromas: Camphor, eucalyptus, pine
Metal: Lead, gold
Tarot Card: The Universe

Myth: Saturn, Cronus, any Father archetype like Father Time. Saturn's common mythology was that he ate his children and then was forced to disgorge them by the one son (Jupiter) who managed to deceive his father and get away. Yet, Saturn also was said to have ruled over the mythological "Golden Age" and was purported to be a fair and just ruler that brought life into balance.

In the birth chart: Saturn is best known as the planet of lessons, limitations, boundaries, restrictions, karma, what holds us back, what holds us down, father, authority, structure, and systems. Saturn is the planet in our chart that tells us where we have to work hard this lifetime. It tells us the area of life in which we must focus concentrated attention, must know this area, must endure and persevere in this area. It is the area and way in which we will connect with the world since Saturn defines our ability and understanding of our culture, our society and the world at large. Saturn tells us if we will fit in or not. It tells us where our deepest ambitions lie, what we feel we need to accomplish, and what we have to finish. Since in reality there are no limitations — everything being energy — then Saturn, I think is the planet that teaches us where we limit ourselves. It shows, sometimes not so gently, how our belief systems and thought patterns limit our experience of reality. The whole purpose of Saturn ultimately is about getting us free — but the way it manifests is through showing us where we are in bondage.

Exercise: Saturn

Since Saturn likes organization and goals, an exercise that supports looking at your priorities can be good Saturn work. Write down all of the things you want to accomplish in the next year. Systematically prioritize this list by comparing each item singularly with every other item. For example, if the first objective on your list is to finish grad school and the second item is to buy a house and the third item is to develop build and support your community, look at whether finishing grad school is more important that buying a house. Then look at whether finishing grad school is more important than building community. Then look at whether buying a house is more important to you than building community. When you have done this with an entire list of objectives, you may be surprised at the clarity and awareness this simple exercise can bring. (And Saturn loves clarity and awareness).

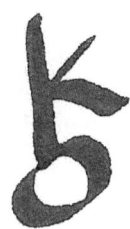

Chiron

Universal Law:

The second law of thermodynamics states that an isolated system will always move from a state of relative order to a state of relative disorder until maximum relative disorder is achieved. The state of maximum relative disorder is thermal equilibrium. So, we move from order to disorder in order to achieve equilibrium, or balance, or harmony. In other words, the path to achieving harmony or equilibrium is to allow chaos, to allow disorder, to allow the unknown.

Chiron allows us to be in the unknown. Chiron supports us in our process from "knowing", from being able to detect and measure through the use of our five senses into the "unknown", the place of trust, allowing and faith, the place of equilibrium. Chiron in the natal chart shows us where we have concretized a belief in life that no longer serves us. Chiron in the natal chart shows us where our wound is—where our state of dis-equilibrium is—where we are out of balance. This area is where we have placed too much significance, control and order. The sign and house and aspects tell us where in our lives we need to let go of a past misconception of life and how it works.

General Associations: Healing, wounding, the ability for us to heal ourselves, teaching, medicine, the bridge between the conscious and unconscious, the body-mind-spirit connection

Rules: Virgo   Detriment: Pisces   Exaltation: Sagittarius   Fall: Leo

Cycle: 51 years to move through the entire zodiac

Discovered: 1977

Astronomical: Is considered a planetoid, a small planet, its size is just a bit smaller than Pluto

Medical Rulerships: The immune system, the body's innate ability to heal itself

Herbs: Astragalus root, medicinal mushrooms   Colors: Gray, silver

Note: E flat
Gems: Sugilite, celestite

Aromas: Benzoin
Tarot Card: The Hanged Man

Myth: Chiron was a Centaur-god who taught medicine to the other gods. A stray arrow wounded him and rather than live forever like gods do, he chose to become mortal so he could die and be released from eternal pain.

In the birth chart: Chiron tells us where some deep and old wounds are. It points to where we have healing to do. We may experience this part of our life as being in crisis, especially until we are 51 years old. The placement of Chiron also tells us about our ability to heal others and ourselves.

By Transit: Chiron can awaken us through crisis so that we make a deeper connection with that which is unseen. Chiron can open an old wound that has not healed completely so that completion can occur.

Chiron return: At about age 51, Chiron returns to its natal position. This is a time when our healing abilities come into fullness. We realize patterns and can move out of the stage of karmic completions into wisdom. The body-mind-spirit connection opens up to new levels.

Exercise: Chiron

For tuning into Chiron, explore through writing how you feel wounded in life.

What do you think is your core wound?

How in your life have you healed, worked with or compensated for this wound?

Explore new ways to heal.

If your Chiron is in:	Consider working with these healing modalities:
Aries	movement therapy, play therapy, energy work, vibrational medicine
Taurus	massage, chiropractic adjustments, herbs, essential oils, mud baths, facials
Gemini	acupuncture, energy work, talk therapy, journal writing
Cancer	emotional release through counseling and therapy
Leo	self-empowerment workshops, dance, expressive arts therapies, situational comedies
Virgo	nutritional supplements and vitamins, herbs, diet, daily lifestyle changes, massage, becoming a healing practitioner of some sort, yoga
Libra	talk therapy, vision work, essential oils, flower essences, one-on-one counseling
Scorpio	movement therapy, gestalt counseling, any in-depth emotional release work, shamanic journeying
Sagittarius	vibrational medicines, flower essences, meditation, studying healing techniques
Capricorn	chiropractic adjustments, massage, somatic therapy
Aquarius	acupuncture, energy work, healing work done in a group, homeopathy
Pisces	group therapeutic processes, spiritually-oriented counseling, meditation, music therapy, yoga

Uranus

Universal Law:
Energy is mass. All matter is made up of energy. It's all energy.

Ohm's Law: Current in a circuit is directly proportional to the applied potential difference V and inversely proportional to the resistance R of the circuit. [8]

Uranus loves change. She wants things to change all the time. In mythology, Uranus is father of Saturn but for some reason I always think of Uranus as a She. So indulge me, please. Uranus rules our energy body—that field of energy around us that emanates and affects the world around us. Uranus tells us it's all energy so anything can change and will change. Uranus wants us to feel and know our energy bodies—that body of light that is in us and surrounds us. She wants us to empower our energy bodies and use them to heal and release. Uranus wants freedom—freedom to do and be anything. She says anything is possible even if you don't believe and if you need a reminder I'll make something happen you won't forget. Uranus reminds us that we live on a fragile changing planet that needs release and change itself. Uranus does not like and has no need for boundaries, integrity, honesty or limitations. If it does not work, change it, and keep changing. Everything is a repercussion of everything else. Since it's all energy, we can step into and out of our bodies, the planet and the third dimension. And if it is all energy, then nothing is good or bad. The only thing she does not like is resistance. Uranus has no patience for resistance. Try to block Uranus and she shakes it up even harder. Uranus rules electricity and works like electricity. She has great energy if we magnetize it to us. The current that can come through us depends on the degree of our resistance and ability to surrender.

What Uranus likes: Change, joy, freedom, intelligence, thinking outside the box, creativity

What Uranus dislikes: Resistance, apathy, lethargy

General Associations: Unpredictable, change, electricity, energy, erratic-ness, aliveness, excitement, freedom, individuality, spontaneity, creativity—especially intellectual, out-of-control, awakening, intuition, the unconventional, social reform, revolution, eccentricity, inventions

Rules: Aquarius   Detriment: Leo   Exaltation: Scorpio   Fall: Taurus

Cycle: Takes approximately 7 years to move through a sign, 84 years to move through the entire zodiac

The Planets – Uranus

Discovered: March 13, 1781 by William Herchel, amateur astronomer in England, coincides with French and American Revolutions, the Industrial Revolution, Mary Wollstonecraft's *A Vindication of the Rights of Women*, discovery of electricity

Astronomical: Rotational axis tilts at 55 degrees—rotates on its side, has a ring of dense particulate matter, many moons

Medical Rulership: Nervous system, especially in the electrical impulses which pass between the nerve cells, the actual impulses that cross nerve synapses, quick culmination and quick release, spasms, sudden onset illnesses, cramps, ruptures, seizures, restlessness, anterior pituitary—regulates the production of cortisol, growth hormone, the gonadal steroids, thyroxin, prolactin, and probably others; Uranus adds a suddenness to the onset of illness.

Vitamins: Magnesium, manganese

Herbs: Borage, raspberry leaf, vervain, valerian (kava, skullcap, gingko)

Color: Blue, electric blue, silver

Note: A

Gems: Lapis lazuli, sapphire, aquamarine, amber

Aromas: Chamomile, marjoram

Metal: Uranium

Tarot Card: the Tower

Higher Octave of Mercury: Uranus is about higher mind, Mercury being about lower mind

Myth: Born from the Earth and lover to the Earth, fathered the Cyclops and the Titans, was castrated by Saturn his son, his genitals thrown into the ocean gave birth to Venus, he then became the Sky God.

In the birth chart: House describes the area of life where we are bound to be making many changes throughout our life, an area of instability, where we express ourselves in original ways

By Transit: Uranus awakens and enlivens any planet or point in the chart in which it transits. It most surely offers us the opportunity for movement, for change in the particular area being aspected. Often the change happens suddenly or in an unexpected way. Opening to change, instigating it, and creating space are all ways to work with Uranus. Holding on to something that has become lifeless and stagnant, clinging to that which is holding us back and refusing to change are all responses to Uranus transitions that basically do not work very well.

Uranus Opposition: At 40, Uranus comes to its opposition point where it is awakened. At this point in our lives, we can channel energy in our body in a new way, can open up to having energy in our body more intensely and can accept ourselves as an agent of change in our own lives. We have the opportunity to realize at a deep level that change is life and life is change. We can no longer feel victim to change happening around us but can see ourselves as the cause, the root and the catalyst of change in our lives. When we refuse to acknowledge this transition by continuing to try to control our lives, clinging to outmoded ways and convention, we may experience break down, break up and burn out. Uranus almost always makes its presence known.

Exercise: Uranus

For exploring Uranus, deep breath work is wonderful. Think about how you deal with change in your life. Write about a time when you felt completely and utterly out of control. Go on a roller coaster ride. Take a chance and do something that excites you. What could you do that would take you out of your everyday life and propel you into a new arena—something that is a little scary or a lot scary—but something that puts you on your edge. Uranus is all about dealing with excitement.

Neptune

Universal Law:
Everything is interconnected.

What Neptune likes: Meditation, out-of-body experiences, love, kindness, generosity
What Neptune dislikes: Pettiness, jealousy, envy, small-mindedness, hoarding, clinging, fear

General Associations: Visions, dreams, fantasy, imagination, inspiration, idealism, spirituality, Divine Love, confusion, music, art, poetry, meditation, yoga, all things that bring us into higher states of consciousness, drugs, alcohol, the ocean, mystery, the invisible, Grace

Rules: Pisces   Detriment: Virgo   Exaltation: Cancer   Fall: Capricorn

Cycle: 165 years to move through the entire zodiac

Discovered: September 23, 1846 by Johann Galle, a German astronomer

Astronomical: Has 2 known moons, mass is 17 times that of Earth, density is 40% of Earth's, temperature is -330° F

Medical Rulerships: Cerebral-spinal fluid, pineal gland, lymphatic system, parts of nervous system that are receptive to psychic impressions, human aura, diffusion, misdiagnosis, masked symptoms, drug sensitivity, weakness, atony (flabby muscle tone), thymus gland, spleen, infections and poisons, toxicity, weakness, drug addiction, coma, poison, lowered immune function

Vitamins and Minerals: Vitamin C, Vitamin A, zinc, potassium
Herbs: Plantain, mugwort
Colors: Blue-violet, lavender, aquamarine, sea-green
Note: B
Gems: Amethyst, fluorite
Aromas: Clary sage, myrrh, frankincense
Metal: Platinum, Neptunium
Tarot Card: The Aeon—"the more that I know that I don't know, the closer I am to the divine"; Judgment (The Moon in tarot is attributed to Pisces)
Higher Octave of Venus: Neptune is about Divine Love, Venus is about Human Love

Myth: Lord of the Oceans, brother to Jupiter and Pluto. In Greek Mythology the Universe was divided into three parts, the Underworld, the heavens and the Seas which were divided among the three brothers. Neptune married a mortal, Leucipe, and had ten sons, the oldest of which was Atlas. In Roman mythology, Neptune's wife is Salacia, the goddess of Salt Water. Neptune ruled Atlantis. In Hindu mythology, Neptune is Narayani, an incarnation of Vishnu.

In the birth chart: The house in which Neptune resides describes the area of life where we are constantly working with our perceptions of reality, where we may get lost in fantasy, and experience delusions and disorientation, an area where there is some confusion. It is the area to which we are asked to surrender in order for clarity to reveal itself, the area where we are more sensitive to the unseen or invisible forces.

Neptune offers us inspiration and vision. It is the planet that points the way to our most idealized version of ourselves and life in general. It represents our dreams, our deepest longings and our most unrealistic expectations. The work of Neptune is to offer us a vision of what is possible without necessarily offering us a way to make it happen. The manifestation part is the work of Saturn, or possibly Venus and Mars.

By Transit: Whenever someone tells me they are feeling confused about some thing in their life, I look for Neptune. Is it transiting some planet in their natal chart? Most times it is. Neptune offers us the opportunity to reflect, to meditate on, to dream about, to open up to greater inspirations, that planetary energy which it is transiting. Often it is difficult to make decisions during a Neptune transit and indeed it may not be a good time to make a decision. Instead it is a wonderful time to be creative, to envision, to write, to imagine.

Exercise: Neptune

In order to tune into Neptune, do what inspires you to allow your imagination to roam free. Listen to poetry. Read inspirational literature. Listen to music that uplifts and soothes your soul. Dance. Sing. Spend time at the ocean or near any body of water.

If your Neptune is in:	The group of souls you came in with are spiritually aligned through:
Aries (2026 - 2038)	A group of souls born to move the whole divine connection business out of the divine connection box. (We'll just have to wait and see what these guys do.)
Taurus (2038 - 2051)	A group of souls who bring it all down and in—what those Neptune in Aries folks instigate.
Gemini (2051 - 2065)	A group of souls here to assist with the integration and flow of a sense of interconnectedness among all life.
Cancer (1901 - 1916)	A group of souls here to experience a divine connection through a sense of place, a calling for home and a deep and sincere connection to family.
Leo (1916 - 1929)	A group of souls with a charismatic and dramatic connection to God, a higher power, a divine connection, etc. A group of souls whose experiences support a direct and intimate connection to a divine order.
Virgo (1929 - 1943)	A group of souls here to practice service as a spiritual path and teach and experience the need for a steady practice that brings one into attunement with a larger picture.
Libra (1943 - 1956)	A group of souls here to be in loving relationship and understanding. They are here to teach and experience the importance of support and intimacy on any spiritual path.
Scorpio (1956 - 1970)	A group of souls who are here to realize the significance of the emotional body in any path of higher learning and spiritual wisdom. The role of cleansing, clearing and experiencing the psyche are brought forth both experientially and as a teaching.
Sagittarius (1970 - 1984)	A group of souls who have the purpose of studying and mastering the ancient and esoteric wisdom teachings. A group of visionaries here to usher in a new vision of both science and spirituality and bridge the perceptual gap between the two.
Capricorn (1984 - 1998)	A group of souls who is called to organize and catalyze the structures needed for the survival of the previous group of soul's teachings to be assimilated into every day life.
Aquarius (1998 - 2011)	A group of souls who are here to have a direct connection to the energetic realms of our interconnectedness and have the abilities to make energetic healing easily accessible.
Pisces (2011 - 2026)	A group of souls born with a deep and abiding connection to Neptune, the unseen realm of spirit and the all—abiding love that is experienced in these realms. This is a group of souls who are here to love and be love.

Pluto

Universal Law:
Everything is evolving. Everything is changing all the time.

Pluto rules death and underworld, but make no mistake. Pluto wants us to live — live life to the fullest. Pluto wants us to taste all the riches of the world — but without attachment. Pluto wants us to understand that we are just visiting and life is short and tenuous. Pluto reminds us that death is right around the corner — so live — Now! Experience everything. Let go of anything that gets in the way. Pluto actually has purpose and intention. He does not long for suffering or misery — those are old notions of hell. Pluto wants us to lose the attachments that are creating the suffering in our lives. Pluto is all about alleviating suffering — and showing us how we are creating our own suffering. Pluto wants us to take this life seriously — wants us to appreciate being given a body — it isn't always easy to get one you know. Pluto helps us unload our burdens — helps us to stop taking on so much baggage. You can't take it with you — is Pluto's motto.

General Associations: Our desire to evolve, transformation, death, the underworld, sexuality, power, where we are letting go, release, magic, shamanism, significant change, upset, destruction, violence, profound shifts, volcanoes, taboos, descent, spirits, ancestors

Rules: Scorpio   Detriment: Taurus   Exaltation: none   Fall: none

Cycle: Its orbit takes 248 years. A complete rotation takes 6 days and 9 hours

Astronomical: Diameter is approximately 3,700 miles, about that of Mercury. No satellites. Moves very slowly — about 10,000 miles per hour (vs. the Earth which moves at about 110,000 miles per hour). Temp = -360°F. Its orbit is very elliptical and is at 17° to the orbital plane. Sometimes it orbits outside of Neptune and sometimes inside of Neptune. Discovered in 1929 in Arizona.

Medical Rulerships: Bowels, reproductive system, creative and regenerative forces and processes, balance between anabolic and catabolic phases of metabolism, life and death, transformation of cells, metabolism, genetics, deterioration, enzyme production, endocrine system, hereditary diseases, malformation, malignancy, bacterial infections, amputation

Vitamins: E, selenium
Herbs: Ginseng, dong quai, damiana, partridge berry
Foods: Wheat germ, cold-pressed oils, kelp, medicinal mushrooms
Colors: Violet, black
Note: E
Gems: Obsidian, jet, pearl
Aromas: Pennyroyal, sage
Metal: Plutonium

Tarot Card: Death
Higher Octave of Mars: Mars is about human desire, Pluto is about the desire of humanity to evolve
Occupations: Shamans, caretakers, miners, underground workers, spies, detectives, researchers, physical and psychic healers, criminals
Day of the Week: none

Myth: The God of the Underworld. Shiva to the Hindus. A god of destruction. Most noted for abducting Persephone and carrying her to the underworld where her mother Demeter pleaded with Jupiter to save her daughter. Jupiter conceded but on the way up Persephone ate the pomegranate seeds which means that she must live with Pluto for half of the year and her mother for the other half.

In the birth chart: Where we are deeply letting go. Our desire to evolve and to deeply change is where Pluto is in the birth chart. We often find that the house in which we find Pluto is the area where we must do the most significant emotional work and where we can find the deepest peace if we are willing to do that work. Pluto in the chart shows us where we are called to evolve. The sign that Pluto is in is a generational sign since it was in that sign for around ten years. The sign of Pluto has less significance in the natal chart than the house in which Pluto resides.

By Transit: Pluto is one of the most significant planets to watch for by transit. It indicates deep and profound changes. It may resonate to a natal planet for over a year giving us time to make deep and lasting changes. It often indicates a time of letting go, of separation, of old ways being destroyed and in the most extreme examples death of a loved one or death of a dream. Pluto usually crosses a natal planet at least three times. The first time through is the destruction or the calling. Then a period of wasteland, of nothingness, of emptiness, of not knowing. The final transit signifies a rebirth, a rebuilding, a totally new way of being, a healing. Pluto begs us to go be alone. It wants us to go willingly to our grief place. Often during Pluto transits we must let go and surrender. We must cry and grieve. The more willing we are to be alone the easier and the quicker will be Pluto's work.

Exercise: Pluto

With Pluto we are learning all about letting go. I often encourage people who are going through a Pluto transit to initiate the letting go process by doing some house clearing. Look at your possessions and see if it is time to let go of something. Give it away, burn it, sell it. Clear out things in your life that may be holding energy that wants to be released. If there is a relationship you want to let go of or a situation or a habit, take something that represents that person, that thing, that habit and get rid of it. Practice the grieving process. Feel all the feelings that go along with releasing that object.

Earth

Universal Law:
The laws of gravity (which are always changing).

To honor our own planet, Gaia, our mother, is to take care of her, relate to her as a living entity, and enjoy the abundance she offers us. The Earth in our chart shows us where to ground, find home and what our particular path of stewardship of this planet is. The earth in our natal chart tells us what our role is in creating a beautiful world to live. Gaia wants us to acknowledge and tend to nature, the wilderness, our gardens, plants, and all living things on this planet (and that includes rocks as I understand it).

General Associations: Groundedness, abundance, stewardship, connection to life, home

Esoteric Ruler: Sagittarius[4]

Cycle: 365.24 days to get around the Sun and 1 day to rotate on its axis, so that every 1461 days the Earth gets around the Sun 4 times

Astronomical: Average distance from the Sun is 93 million miles, tilt on axis is 23.45 degrees, temperatures run from –128 F to +136 F, 70% of Earth is covered by water

Medical Rulerships: Simply being human on a living planet

Vitamins: Iodine, copper
Herbs: Wherever the entire plant is used, especially comfrey and dandelion
Foods: Root vegetables
Colors: Green and blue
Myth: All creation myths

Gems: All quartz gems
Aromas: All aromas
Occupations: Anything to do with preserving and serving this planet

---

[4] As the Earth is rarely used in interpretation in western astrology, there are no traditional rulers.

In the birth chart: The Earth is always opposite the Sun. The Sun is our life force and the Earth is how we use our life force. Earth in the natal chart shows us how to direct our life force so that we can be productive, efficient and in kinship with all life. The Earth in the chart shows us where and how we can be most resourceful. It represents the sustaining of energy, the caring for our selves and the ability to tap into energy resources in order to fulfill our life task. The energy of the Sun is here to be used with gratitude, with wisdom and with care. Conserving our life energy — Earth acts as the capacitor in the circuit in the way that the Earth stores energy at its core and through its plant life.

By Transit: The Earth moves quickly and transits our charts on the same day as the Sun. While the Sun is allowing us greater life energy, the Earth is asking us to use it wisely.

Exercise: Earth

To learn about your Earth: Take time out in nature — go for the wildest most natural place you can find. Notice what comes to you. Notice how you walk and how you work with the Earth. In everyday life, notice how much waste you generate. Notice how well you care for your environment and where there is room for improvement. Make correlations with how much life energy you have. Holding on to energy is also a way of not having it.

The Moon's Nodes

There are two nodes of the Moon, the North Node and the South Node.

The South Node of the Moon is the entry point of the soul into the body. The South Node represents our past lives, what we come into this life with, our predisposition, what is familiar to us. The South Node is the known. Contained in the South Node is the story of our past. It is our myth, our old life story that we are living out of and leaving behind. We gather and use the gifts that we bring into this life, yet we must move away from the familiar into the unknown.

The North Node is the unknown. It is the unfamiliar and the longing of the soul. The North Node is the point in the chart we are moving toward. We are embracing the North Node, accepting it and incorporating it into our lives. Where the North Node is, we are being asked to develop. We are the beginner. It is the area of life in which we feel the most uneasy and out-of-sorts. As we focus more and more on the North Node, our soul feels happier, we radiate more and our soul more deeply connects with our physical existence.

North Node
Stones: Hessonite, brown tourmaline
Metal: Silver

South Node
Stones: Cat's eye, lapis lazuli, tiger's, turquoise, agate
Metal: Gold

Exercise: The Moon's Nodes

Find the South Node in your chart. What sign and house is it in?
Write a basic description of the sign and house.
Take a look at your life prior to your Saturn return—until you were about 29 years old. How does the focus of your life at that time mirror your South Node?

Find the North Node in your chart. What sign and house is it in?
Write a description of that sign and house.
Describe your ideal situation for that particular house. Example: If your North Node is in the fourth house, describe your ideal home and family situation. If your North Node is in the sixth house, describe your perfect day, routine or job.

Note the sign the North Node is in. How can you develop that sign's qualities more in your life? How can that feed your soul?

North Node (South Node):	Explore:	Gift available to you at birth:	Tendency you are leaving behind:
Aries (Libra)	Being more spontaneous and brave. Speaking your mind more. Taking the initiative in life.	Ability to listen. Ease of being in relationship. Being able to see both sides of an issue.	Being overly absorbed in your partner's life. Neglecting your own interests.
Taurus (Scorpio)	Being more stable. Working harder and more physically.	Being honest, clear and direct. Being powerful and intense. Able to be emotionally present.	Being overly dramatic or intense without taking responsibility.
Gemini (Sagittarius)	Being more flexible and adaptable. Paying more attention to what is going on around you.	Being able to journey and travel. A pleasure in learning and growing.	Being too extravagant or excessive.
Cancer (Capricorn)	Being more nurturing and caring. Being more sensitive and emotional.	Good organizational skills. Responsible and able to systemize and give structure.	Being too controlling, ambitious and/or domineering.
Leo (Aquarius)	Being more of a leader, more brave, more self-expressive.	Out of the box thinking. Intellectual creativity. Inventiveness.	Being too aloof, too mental, too rebellious.
Virgo (Pisces)	Being more attentive to the details. Being more in the moment. Living simpler and more in the body.	Kindness and compassion. Sensitivity. Open psychic channels. Empathy.	Being too dreamy or lost. Being too invested in what others feel or think about you or anything.
Libra (Aries)	Being more interactive with others. Relating more. Listening more.	Courage. Risk-taking. A sense of adventure.	Being too brash and inconsiderate of others.

North Node (South Node):	Explore:	Gift available to you at birth:	Tendency you are leaving behind:
Scorpio (Taurus)	Being more open to transformation and deep change. Being more emotional and intense.	Ability to work hard. Tenacity. Strong connection to Earth.	A sense of being burdened.
Sagittarius (Gemini)	Being more exploratory. Being more open.	Ability to multi-task, think many thoughts at once and take care of what is right in front of you.	Being too scattered.
Capricorn (Cancer)	Being more responsible and in integrity.	Ability to be nurturing and sensitive. Being in touch with your feelings.	Being overly needing of other's attention.
Aquarius (Leo)	Being more aware of the energy of the group and community. Being more touch with unconventional ideas and rhythms.	Ability to lead and express yourself.	Needing to stand out. Being overly demanding of attention.
Pisces (Virgo)	Being more empathetic and caring, more giving and loving.	Ability to be clear and present in the moment. Being in touch with one's body and physical reality.	Being overly demanding of perfection.

Rulerships

Each of the planets have signs in which they resonate most deeply or struggle most intensely. The planets each have their own energy and this energy operates more easily or with more difficulty depending on the sign it is in. Saturn likes to slow things down and bring things into physical reality. It is not so happy in the process-oriented sign of Cancer. Jupiter likes to expand so it is happy in the anything-is-possible sign of Sagittarius, while Jupiter's joy of expression does not resonate so well with signs that are oriented toward integrity and accountability like Virgo and Capricorn.

Each planet has a sign that it is particularly fond of and we say that that planet *rules* that sign or is in its *dignity* when in that sign. The *detriment* is often the opposite sign to the ruling sign and is the least favorable sign for that planet. Where a planet is *exalted*, it is also happy, but not as happy as when the planet is in its ruling sign. The planet in *fall* is in the sign opposite the exalted sign and is likewise not happy but not as weakened as if the planet is in its detriment.

Sometimes a planet is described as being strengthened in its rulership and exaltation and weakened in its detriment and fall. The rulerships are very important to memorize and know. They can be very helpful in understanding a person's strengths and challenges.

PLANET	RULER	DETRIMENT	EXALTATION	FALL
Sun	Leo	Aquarius	Aries	Libra
Moon	Cancer	Capricorn	Taurus	Scorpio
Mercury	Gemini, Virgo	Sagittarius, Pisces	Aquarius	Leo
Venus	Taurus	Scorpio	Pisces	Virgo
Mars	Aries	Libra	Capricorn	Cancer
Jupiter	Sagittarius, Pisces	Gemini, Virgo	Cancer	Capricorn
Saturn	Capricorn	Cancer	Libra	Aries
Chiron	Virgo	Pisces	Sagittarius	Gemini
Uranus	Aquarius	Leo	Scorpio	Taurus
Neptune	Pisces	Virgo	Cancer	Capricorn
Pluto	Scorpio	Taurus	none	none
Earth	Sagittarius	Gemini	none	none

Exercise: Rulerships

Look at all the planets your chart and find planets that are in their ruling sign, detriment, fall and exaltation. How does knowing this information change the way you feel about that planet and part of yourself? How much do you find ease or struggle with that part of yourself and how does that align with that planet's ease or struggle in that sign?

The Houses

The houses are our life divided into twelve sections. Each section while being a separate part is also in relationship to the other parts. Most importantly, there is the relationship between opposing houses. The house on the other side of the chart is a mirror of that house. Neither house can truly be looked at without acknowledging the opposite house—the mirror. In order for us to understand how we function as an individual (1st house) we must also look at how we function in relationship (7th house). In order for us to understand our relationship to the material world we must look at both how we attain (2nd house) and how we give away (8th house). To understand how we communicate, we must look at how we relate to the small picture—what is right in front of us (3rd house) and the big picture (9th house). For clarity about home and family (4th house), we must also look at how we relate to the world—our larger family (10th house). For a look into our mode of self-expression (5th house) we must also look at how we are in groups (11th house). To gain greater perspective on our path of service (6th house) we must also know our relationship to God or Spirit (12th house).

Often people ask me what it means if they do not have any planets in a house. My answer is that it depends. An empty house can mean that you have little or no work to do in that area of life. It can mean that there are no particular issues you are working out in that area. While this may often be the case it is not always. In other words, you can have an empty house of money and still have a lot of money issues. However, I would be looking at other areas in order to understand those money issues. The planets indicate where there is work to do, where we have issues, where we are focusing our attention this life.

The houses always go in the same order. Start at 9 o'clock in the chart. That is the ascendant and the cusp of the first house. From there travel counter clockwise into the second house. Depending on the house calculation system, the houses can vary in size. There are several different house systems, actually sixteen house systems that my computer software calculates. In all of them, the ascendant will be the same. I have seen Porphyry, Whole House and Koch house systems used successfully and know lots of excellent astrologers who use those systems. My first great astrology reading was with Wendy Ashley. She used Placidus, so that is what I started to use. I found it worked and stuck with it.

The Houses

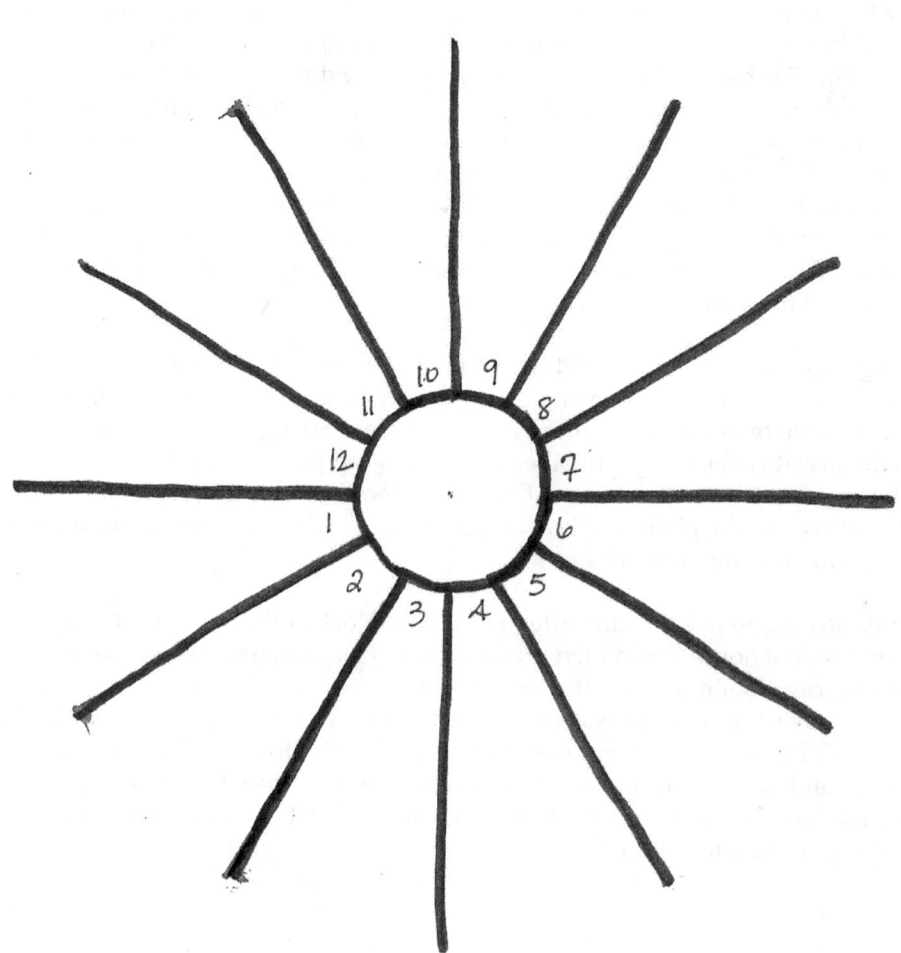

The Houses

Exercise: An Introspective Preview of the Houses

Each of the houses corresponds to an area of life. Think about the following areas in your life without looking at your chart. Write a few sentences. Then read the corresponding chapter. After reading, look at your chart and notice the planets that are in that house. Note any connections you make between that area of life for you and the planets in that house.

1st: Identity. Describe your identity, how you see yourself.

2nd: Resources. Tell about your resources and current state of financial affairs.

3rd: Communication. Describe your communication style.

4th: Home/Family. Describe your home and /or your immediate family.

5th: Self-Expression/Children: Describe how you creatively express yourself or your experience with children.

6th: Work and Health: Describe your work life and your state of health.

The Houses

7th: Partnership: Describe the relationship you are in.

8th: Sex, Death & Rebirth: Describe your relationship with death or sex or transformation.

9th: Exploration (Travel/Higher Education): Describe your traveling life &/or yourself as an explorer.

10th: Life Path/Career: Describe your career life &/or dharma/life path.

11th: Community: Describe your circle of friends/community.

12th: Endings/Spiritual Life: Describe your spiritual life or what you are letting go of.

1st House

In the first house we begin our journey. We start. Whatever is in this house we must know intimately as it is who we are identified with. The first house answers the question, "who am I?" and tells us how important it is for us to know and ask this question.

This is the house of our identity. Planets and signs in this house must be assimilated into our personality and physical well-being. In the first house we decide who we are and how we are going to present ourselves to the world.

What are the planets in your first house (or is it empty)?
What sign is on the cusp of the first house?
This is your ascendant—your rising sign. This is how others see you, how you present yourself to the world. This is your vibrational field, the skin of your soul which others interact with and acknowledge.

2nd House

In the second house, we ground our visions. We examine our values and learn about what is important to us. Planets in the second house are related to material objects—they exist on the material plane, since that is what we are learning about in the 2nd house.

The second house asks the question: "What is important to you? What do you value?" What we value is where we put our energy. What is important to us is what we manifest. The second house offers us answers to our issues of money, resources and land. It is the house that represents our relationship to nature and to the earth we live on.

What are the planets in your second house (or is it empty)?
What is the sign on the cusp of this house? Does it reflect your values?

3rd House

In the 3rd house, we are learning our own particular style of connecting. How we communicate and set up our daily lives is part of this step. We are finding our voice and style. In the third house we explore how we speak, write and understand language. Our relationship with our siblings is reflected in this house as well. The planets and signs in this house describe the way we express ourselves through language, our ability to be heard and to listen to others.

What are the planets in your third house (or is it empty)?
What is the sign on the cusp of this house? Does it reflect the way you communicate with others?

4th House

In the 4th house, we are laying the foundation for our work in the world. We are creating our home or finding our home. We are beginning to relate to others. The first people we usually relate to are our family and thus the 4th house is the house of family.

The fourth house is the house of roots and of our ancestors (along with the 8th house). How we relate to ourselves shows up in the fourth house. Our desire and ability to accept intimacy in our lives shows up in the fourth house. While not directly a relationship house, it is an important house to look at when exploring relationship issues since it tells us of our capacity for intimacy and how we feel loved and nurtured.

What are the planets in your fourth house (or is it empty)?
What sign is on the cusp of your fourth house?

5th House

In the 5th house, we are coming out into the world. We recognize our audience and a need to perform. We are finding our mode of creativity and self-expression. We are birthing ourselves into the world. We see that the world exists and it appears to exist for us. We fall in love with love. This is the house of creative self-expression. It is the house of putting ourselves out into the world. Planets in this house show us what we need to express in the world. Leadership potential can show up in this house. How we fall in love shows up in the fifth house. This house shows us our relationship to children; having children, our own children, working with children and playing.

What are the planets in your fifth house (or is it empty)?
What sign rules your fifth house?
How do these planets and/or sign reflect your avenue of creative expression?
What are you feelings and/or experiences of having children? Is this reflected in this house?

6th House

In the 6th house we recognize that the world wants something from us and that it is a need that we have to give of ourselves. We look for our path of service. We begin to create our daily lives around what is needed from us. Our routines, our breath, our ability to be present in the moment all come under the sixth house. This is the last house below the horizon and so we are completing our work of developing the self and preparing for the work of relating. We are developing a sense of humility and sincerity. The sixth house tells us about how we have incarnated into a body and our relationship to having a body.

What are the planets in your sixth house (or is it empty)?
What sign rules your sixth house?
How do these signs and planets reflect how you feel about your body, your health and your daily work in the world? How much routine do you like? How grounded do you feel in the world in a body? How do you feel about being of service?

7th House

This is the house of the mirror—where we see ourselves in another or in the world. It is the reflection of the self. The 7th house is also about coming out into the world. It is the first house that is above the horizon. It represents what is becoming visible to us in our lives—what can be seen. We cannot see ourselves unless we have a mirror. It is a relationship house—the house of being in a relationship, i.e. doing the work of relationship. The seventh house shows us our relationship to the world—how comfortable we feel with other people. In the seventh house we make contracts and commitments—we set intentions for connections with others.

What are the planets in your seventh house (or is it empty)?
What is the sign on the cusp of the seventh house?
How do the signs and planets reflect your experience of relationships?

8th House

The 8th house is teaching us that unless we look deeply into our nature we cannot move on. We must at this junction acknowledge our mortality—the reality of death. We must dig down deep to experience the heart of matters and find the place where hope is not a fantasy but a natural outcome of seeing in the darkness. The eighth house rules sex, death and rebirth. It also contains money from others, money from inheritances and money from grants. In the eighth house we are bringing our relationships into fulfillment. From the commitment and intention of the seventh house, we go to the depths of the potential of our relationship in the eighth house. Here we experience the mystical union. We transcend normal reality and find passion and power. The eighth house wants us to feel power and empowered.

What are the planets in your eighth house (or is it empty)?
What is the sign on the cusp of the eighth house?
How do these signs and planets reflect how you experience sex, death, rebirth, transformation, money from others, power and deep mystical union with partners?

9th House

In the 9th house, we come out into the light. We search for truth. We open to the world and deepen our study. We get serious about our path. We are close to the pinnacle, the apex. We journey and quest. We search to find ourselves, our world and our universe. We look for God, for love and for answers. We explore and educate ourselves. We search for meaning.

What are the planets in your ninth house (or is it empty)?
What is the sign on the cusp?
How do these signs and houses reflect your experience of travel, higher education, quests for truth, searches for meaning and spiritual pilgrimages?

10th House

We are at the peak expression of our path. The world is shouting in our ears and we must work very hard. Bodies in the 10th tell us the nature of what the world is demanding from us. We cannot hide. In the tenth house we find planets that tell us about our work in the world — the task we were given to do here in a body on planet earth. Our dharma can be read in the tenth house. It is not always what we do for money. It is our vocation. It is our calling. The tenth house reflects our need for recognition, respect and authority in the world. It shows our relationship to fame, success and status.

What are the planets in your tenth house (or is it empty)?
What is the sign ruling the cusp of the tenth house?
How do these signs and planets reflect your calling, vocation and work in the world?

11th House

We have recognized and accomplished our goals in the 10th and can now begin to enjoy the camaraderie and connection of others. We share openly our gifts. We need to feel free. In the eleventh house we find our community, our connection to that group of souls and our relationships within that group. We accept our place in the world. We experience our gifts and look into the future. We find our friends in the eleventh—our relationship to them, their significance in our lives and our need for them. Community is the eleventh house—our communal experience of life.

What are the planets in your eleventh house (or is it empty)?
What is the sign on the cusp of the eleventh?
How do these signs and houses reflect your experience with friends and community?

12th House

In the 12th house, we are letting go of all attachment to our work, our path and our goals. This is an area where we are searching for a larger experience-the freedom and bliss of spirit. We are moving into solitude and isolation and must leave the world behind. What is in this house is often hidden from us and hard to get at. Only in quietude and solitude can we recognize what is here for us. This is often called the house of undoing since whatever is in this house must be let go of—undone. This is the house of mysticism, higher love and devotion. In the twelfth we dissolve into the world, we release what we have known as "mine" or "ours". Here we rest. Here we lie down and let some higher force, some cosmic experience of the Divine take over. In the twelfth we learn to truly relax and smell the roses. Since we must live in the unknown, the more we accept the total out-of-control-ness of life, the easier anything in the twelfth house is.

What are the planets in your twelfth house (or is it empty)?
What is the sign on the cusp of the 12th house?
How do these planets and signs reflect on your experience of spirit, the invisible and what you are releasing this lifetime?

Exercise: Nodes in Houses

In order to explore the houses, look at the houses of your nodes.

Find the South Node in your chart.
My South Node is in the sign of _____ and in the _____ house.
Write a history of your life focusing on the area of life (house) in which your South Node resides.

Find the North Node in your chart.
My North Node is in the sign of _____ and in the _____ house.
Find music that resonates with the sign of your North Node.
While playing the music, make a collage that reflects the area of life of your North Node.
Envision what you would like this area of life to be like. Write down your vision.

Music suggestions:

Element of North Node	Music suggestions
Fire (Aries, Leo, Sagittarius)	Hard rock, classic rock Alternative rock, Metal, Punk Bold classical, like Music for Royal Fireworks by Handel or Rite of Spring by Stravinsky
Earth (Taurus, Virgo, Capricorn)	Indian Chanting Mid-eastern music African drumming Hip hop Reggae
Air (Gemini, Libra, Aquarius)	Any classical music Folk music Jazz
Water (Cancer, Scorpio, Pisces)	Pop music to evoke emotion Opera Rhythm and Blues New Age

Putting the Planet, Sign and House Together

Planets = the energy, the characters
Signs = how the energy manifests
Houses = in what area of life the energy manifests
Aspects = the relationship between the energies

I often wish there was a great formula for this. As is, I feel like the formula I have is only fairly adequate, if that. I offer it to you as a starting point on your journey.

- Each planet is in a sign and in a house.
- Take each planet as the noun, the subject of the sentence.
- The sign describes the planet. Take the sign as an adjective of the noun.
- Examples: Mars in Scorpio=intensely driven.
- Mercury in Virgo=skillful or critical communicator.
- Then add the house as the area of life in which this particular form operates.
- Examples: Mars in Scorpio in the 10th house=intensely driven toward success in the world, Mars in Scorpio in the 2nd=intensely driven to obtain personal resources,
- Mercury in Virgo in the 7th=skillful communicator in relationships, Mercury in Virgo in the 1st=projected self-image as a skillful communicator.

It does not always work out as easily as these examples and we need to play with definitions. That is why it is so important to understand the underlying concepts behind what the signs and planets mean. When we can relate to the energy of the signs and planets, we are freer and more able to express their essence as it is relative to the person or situation.

Example: Let's take Mars in Scorpio in the 10th.

While "intensely driven toward success in the world" is not a bad definition and probably describes many people with this aspect, it most likely states the obvious to the person and leaves them little place to go with it. If we go more deeply into who Mars is mythically and look at the element and modality of Scorpio and the overall placement of the 10th house in the chart—we can glean a deeper meaning.

Mars was a God of War. He charged into battle. He led troops. But in all of his myths, he only killed one person. He was not much of a murderer (at least as far as the gods go). He was brave and courageous. He represents that instinct to go forward, to charge ahead, to not hesitate, to live for the moment. He is the planet of "Carpe Diem". Where Mars is located in the chart, we must act, must assert ourselves.

Scorpio is a fixed water sign. That puts it in the emotional realm. The fixed energy says it is a receiver, a sign that draws in energy from the surroundings and coalesces it. I often think that Scorpio has a reputation for being so hard to deal with because it is constantly taking in the emotions from the surrounding environment, processing those feelings and spitting out the impurities that would destroy them. So we get back the impurities to deal with ourselves.

Mars in Scorpio says this is a person whose ability to be assertive has to do with receiving what is around them, processing this, using it and moving forward with it. This person can use the available energy around them to take action in the direction they desire. There is a power in this person, an impressive assertiveness that can obtain and direct resources to the force of their will.

The 10th house is at the top of the chart. It is the culmination, the peak. Planets in the 10th house were high in the sky at birth. They were visible and obvious. They are guiding points. They point to our direction in life—this life. They are what the world calls us to do with this one precious and wild life.

A person with *Mars in Scorpio in the 10th house* is called by the world to take action out of the energy that is available in the environment around them. They are asked by the world to move forward with their ideas, their impulses, and their will. The world offers its energy to the person with Mars in Scorpio so that they will be successful, driven, ambitious, alive, and active in the pursuit of their goals. It is a blessing from the world for them to go forward with their impulses.

See, now we have a description that offers something to the individual. Instead of boxing in the person as being intensely driven toward success, they can see that they have a particular purpose, a particular calling. Each planet is a calling. Each is the world asking something from us—either to learn something, to express something, to be something, to love something, etc.

> *I think it is important, as we learn to interpret the natal chart, to allow for the ever-evolving nature of the individual to be fully expressed. While we can perceive energy patterns and know the repeating cycles of these patterns, our free will can alter our experience and results. The chart offers us a chance to gain perspective, offers us a more expansive view, and can allow us to make decisions freer from the limitations that are so often oppressively placed on us in our society.*

Let's do another example, since that one was so much fun.

Venus in Aries in the 12th

A general definition using the formula might be: She relates courageously or impulsively in seclusion. Okay, so the formula doesn't always work. We can tweak it a bit. Her personal magnetism, assertive in nature, must be overcome. Or, her urge to relate comes from karmic patterns of rashness. Her inner nature is to hide but it is also aggressive? Basically, this is a hard one to describe from a narrow perspective.

Let's pull it apart. *Venus* is our inner nature. How we relate to others is a direct expression of how we relate to ourselves. Venus, mythically, operated on the principle that there is always enough, more than enough, there is always *abundanza* (abundance). While in one relationship, there was always another around the corner. She is the Goddess of Pleasure—pleasure as a gift from the gods—as something divine. Venus is then our ability to experience pleasure, to relate to others and feel prosperous and abundant in all things but especially material things.

Aries, cardinal fire, is the first sign and a symbol of birth. Aries is the spark—the beginning of fire, that which ignites us, that lights us up. It is fire that originates in our center and moves outward, shoots out of us as a gift. It is fire, so it is not processed. It is raw. It is a purely spontaneous act. There is no thought, no hesitation, no withhold. Aries has no manners, no culture, no consideration for others. It exists merely to express itself out into the world without refinement of any form.

The 12th house is not any easy house to explain. It is the house of mystery, of what is hidden, of what is dissolving, of what we are releasing without even knowing it. It is the house of spirituality, not religion. There is nothing organized about the 12th house. Everything in the 12th house must be surrendered. We have no control. It is that place where we are infinitely alone and infinitely connected. It is our experience of God, our experience of Faith, our experience of Divine Love. Sometimes it is called the house of karma. While the entire chart tells us about our karma, the twelfth house is the house where we cannot deny our karma. My own definition of karma is that which we believe, a construct or thought pattern, that contributes to the creation of our reality. I think that we carry these karmas through death and into life again however that may look.

So here is a person, whose experience of pleasure, whose sense of abundance, whose urge to relate lies in the house of "undoing", of what she is letting go of. Not an easy thing to be letting go of—pleasure that is. But what is really happening? What does it really mean to let go of something? Since energy is never lost, letting go simply means to transfer energy elsewhere, opening oneself up to greater pleasure. Perhaps more of an experience of divine pleasure, which is experienced in altered states of consciousness, in moments of spiritual rapture. I would say this person is going for a profound experience of rapture-and she is going for it with gusto, without hesitation, with an impulsive Arian drive. She may experiment with many things—drugs, alcohol (the most readily available altered states in our culture), gurus, Kundalini yoga, music. No matter what she is doing she must "get high" in the way that Ram Dass talks about high. She is passionately moving toward a greater pleasure, a greater love, a higher sense of self. Her inner nature must be spiritually based—must be about relating to a larger presence, must be longing for union. This is a person who can do the spiritual-nun thing or the ashram thing and not feel deprived. It is where her abundance lies.

Real Life Examples:

Barack Obama[5]: Sun in Leo in the 6th house. His identity (Sun) is full of vigor, courage and leadership ability (Leo) in service to others (6th house). Mars in Virgo in the 7th house. Detail-oriented (Virgo) at work (Mars) in partnership with others. Dedicated (Virgo) assertiveness (Mars) in partnerships (7th house).

Steve Jobs[6]: Mercury in Aquarius in the 12th house. His mind (Mercury) works innovatively (Aquarius) in solitude searching for something greater than what can easily be observed (12th house.) Venus in Capricorn in the 11th house. Creativity and passion (Venus) that was organized (Capricorn) in collaboration (11th house). Desire (Venus) to improve and master (Capricorn) new ways of doing things (11th house).

Oscar Wilde[7]: Mars in Sagittarius in the 3rd house. His will force and actions (Mars) were expansive and seeking (Sagittarius) in communication and writing (3rd house). He had an expansive (Sagittarius) way (Mars) of communicating. Oscar Wilde's wit was notable. Mars is often connected to our sense of humor, particularly in connection with Mercury. Oscar Wilde's Mercury is also in the 3rd house, but in Scorpio not Sagittarius. His communication style (Mercury) was deep and penetrating (Scorpio). Mars brought out possibility (Sagittarius) while Mercury brought forth profound emotion and depth (Scorpio). His South Node is also in Scorpio in the 3rd house. South Node in the 3rd supports past lives of spending a lot of time learning many different things but never being recognized for it. South Node in Scorpio suggests past lives of emotional depth and intensity, supporting a deep curiosity. The North Node then is in Taurus in the 9th supporting him in being published and recognized (9th house) in a creative way (Taurus). He would get a solid (Taurus) education (9th house).

Marie Curie[8]: Mercury in Sagittarius in the 11th house. An expansive (Sagittarius) mind (Mercury) thinking innovatively and outside the box (11th house). A mind (Mercury) capable of seeing the big picture (Sagittarius) for the future (11th house). Mars in Scorpio in the 11th house. Intensely (Scorpio) active (Mars) and passionate (Mars in Scorpio) for a cause (11th house). Venus in Scorpio in the 11th house. Deep (Scorpio) lover (Venus) of science (11th house).

---

[5] Barack Obama. 08/04/1961 7:24pm Honolulu, Hawaii 21N18, 157W51 Rated AA

[6] Steve Jobs. 02/24/1955 6:40am San Francisco, California 37N46 122W25 Rated A

[7] Oscar Wilde. 10/16/1854 3:00am Dublin, Ireland 53N20 6W15

[8] Marie Curie. 11/7/1867 10:36am Warsaw, Poland 52N15 21E00 Rated AA

Exercise: Planets in their Sign and House

Describe each of the planets in your chart. Include information about the sign the planet is in, the house the planet is in and the energy of the planet itself.

Sun

Moon

Mercury

Venus

Mars

Jupiter

The Nodes

Saturn

Chiron

Uranus

Neptune

Pluto

The Angles

Ascendant, (ASC)
Descendant (DSC)
Midheaven (MC)
Imum Coeli (IC)

The Angles, as they are not so aptly named, mark the four directions in the chart. The angles are not to be confused with aspects, even if the aspects are technically angles and the angles are technically directions. Alas, we much live with the names as they have come to us through translations, upon translations.

The Angles are the four corners. The Ascendant marks the Eastern horizon, where the Sun rises. The Descendant marks the western horizon, where the Sun sets. The Midheaven marks the highest point the Sun reaches in the day. The Imum Coeli marks the nadir, the lowest point where the Sun shines high on the other side of the world.

Before we go further, let's acknowledge that we are about to enter the movement of the chart. For the past chapters, we have been exploring the chart as a stagnant map holding the planets still in a sign and house. In order to enter the world of the angles, and into the next chapter of the aspects, we have to relate to the way the planets move. The chart is a two-dimensional representation of a three-dimensional system. Add in the aspects and transits and it becomes a four-dimensional system.

The planets move through the signs of the zodiac in a counter-clockwise direction.
The planets move through the houses in a counter-clockwise direction.
The houses move through the zodiac in a clockwise direction.

Look at the chart like a clock face.

At 9 o'clock is the Ascendant. This is where the Sun rises. If the Sun is at 9 o'clock in your chart, then you were born at dawn. Yes—I know it's confusing, since on a compass, 9 o'clock is West. Sigh. In a western-based astrology chart, East is West, West is East, North is South and South is North. At 12 o'clock is the MC. Which is South if you are living in the Northern hemisphere. At 6 o'clock is the DSC. At 4 o'clock is the IC.

The Angles

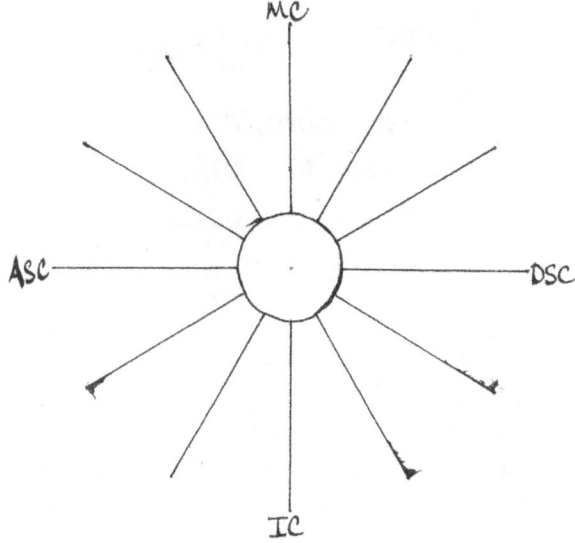

The Ascendant (ASC)

Also known as the Rising Sign, the ascendant is the point of awareness, the entry into the chart. It represents the face we show the world. It is our personality and the way we look. It is how we identify our self, name our self and present our self. In Esoteric astrology, the ascendant represents our spiritual purpose. It is a window into the rest of the chart. The sign on the ascendant describes our personality. Planets near the ascendant show us our true personality.

The Descendant (DSC)

The descendant represents our relationships with others and with the world. It is the point where the planets set. The sign on the descendant takes us within and reflects our light. The sign is the sign we look for in our partners. In the birth chart, planets near the descendant color the nature of our partnerships, both romantic and in business.

The Midheaven (MC)

Up high in the chart, the midheaven tells us about our vocation, the thing the world wants from us. It is the point that is fully visible to others. It tells us the task that we are here on this planet to do. I think of it as our contract with Earth. We get to come here, have a body, experience life and grow spiritually. In return, this world requires something of us and the secret to that requirement lies in understanding the midheaven, the sign and planets near it.

The Imum Coeli (IC)

At the nadir, the bottom of the chart, lies our home, the foundation of our life. The Imum Coeli, the IC, is the point that tells us about what we stand on in life. It is our roots. It is how we find home, what we long for in home and what home means to us. It leads us to understand our family and the issues we have with our family.

It is important to note that planets and signs on the angles appear larger. As they appear larger physically, they take on more meaning and are viewed with greater significance. When we work with the natal chart, we are standing in the center of our own universe and everything is viewed from our own very personal perspective. Objects on the horizon appear larger. The Sun appears to revolve around us. Planets appear to move backwards (retrograde). The Sun and the Moon appear to be the same size. Eclipses appear as if one orb blocks out another. The Moon appears to wax and wane. Appearances, in the case of natal chart astrology, matter.

Exercise: Angles

Angle	Sign & Degree	Planets nearby	Describe your current situation and your ideal situation
ASC			Your appearance
DSC			Your partner

Angle	Sign & Degree	Planets nearby	Describe your current situation and your ideal situation
IC			Your home
MH			Your vocation

Aspects

Aspect: the number of degrees apart two planets or points in space are from each other in relation to the earth (or, potentially, another celestial body)

The number of degrees apart two planets or points are from each other determines their particular relationship—whether these two planets or points work well together, have friction or dance in some other mystical or creative way.

Aspects are the dance of the planets, how two or more planets relate to each other.

While the planets are always in some angular relationship to each other, certain numbers of degrees apart correspond to different types of relationships and therefore different interpretations. For example, the *trine* which is 120 degrees and the *square* which is 90 degrees reflect different relationships and have different interpretations.

The **orb** of an aspect is the range of degrees in which that relationship, that aspect, is applicable and observable. For example, a square aspect, which is 90 degrees, is when two planets are between 82 and 98 degrees apart. The two planets are still considered a square even if they are up to 8 degrees away from being an exact square (90 degrees). This is an *orb* of 8 degrees.

Aspects as Harmonics

One way to look at aspects is to determine the vibration of the aspect (or angle). This vibration is based on the harmonic. The harmonic is the number of times the wheel is divided. The first harmonic is the wheel undivided and represents the conjunction. The wheel divided in half is the second harmonic and includes the conjunction and opposition (0 and 180 degrees). In music, the higher the harmonic the weaker the vibration. So we can take that into astrology to say that the higher the harmonic the weaker the aspect and therefore the smaller the orb we should use. You may notice that the orbs noted here are slightly different than convention.

Aspects

Harmonic	Orb	Aspects	Description
1st	10	Conjunction	Unity, power, direction, focus
2nd	10	Opposition	Polarity, balancing, mirroring
3rd	8	Trine	Strength, gifts, flow
4th	8	Square	Challenge, manifestation, charge
5th	4	Quintile, Bi-quintile	Creativity, magic
6th	3	Sextile, Trine	Connection, groundedness, opportunity
7th	2	Septile, Bi-septile, Tri-septile	Mysticism, vision
8th	2	Semi-square, sesquiquadrate, square, opposition	Stress, change, tension
9th	1	Novile, bi-novile, tri-novile, quart-novile	Completion
10th	1	Quintile, Bi-quintile, deciles, oppositions	Powerful magic of spirit & matter
11th	1	Undeciles	Mastery, ascension
12th	1	Semi-sextile, quincunx, square, trine, opposition	Adjustment
13th	1	Thirteenths (27.7 degrees)	Transformation, higher knowledge

Applying and Separating Aspects

Planets are either moving into or out of a geometric relationship. The two planets are either moving towards the exact aspect or moving out of the exact aspect. When the two planets are moving into or toward the exact degree of the aspect, the aspect is an **applying** aspect. When the two planets have already formed an exact aspect and are moving out of the aspect, the aspect is **separating**.

Applying aspects tend to be more intense the closer they get to exact. Often the relationship between the two planets feels new and unfamiliar. We may experience the aspect as uncomfortable and struggle against it. We may find ourselves needing to learn the hard way. Even trines, which are about gifts and strengths, may show us gifts and strengths that feel awkward to us to use. They are more likely to be talents that we didn't know we had until pushed to recognize them.

Separating aspects tend be experienced as aspects that we already know how to deal with. They tend to be familiar and we may have an already formed pattern for how to deal with the aspect. Challenging aspects tend to be experienced as dynamic and motivating rather than stressful. Aspects that involve talents and gifts tend to be gifts that come to us easily, gifts we know we have and can easily express.

Synodic Cycles and Waxing and Waning Aspects

Every planet has a cyclical relationship to every other planet. The two planets appear to join (appear at the same longitude in the sky) and then they move out of that joining. The faster planet pulls away. From that pulling away, the two planets continue to relate to each other at different angle until once again they join. This cycle is called the Synodic Cycle. There is a Venus-Mars synodic cycle, a Jupiter-Saturn synodic cycle, a Mars-Jupiter synodic cycle, etc. For all of the Planetary Synodic Periods, see chart that follows.

The number of aspects in a harmonic is equal to the number of the harmonic. Within the 8th harmonic are eight aspects—the two planets move into the 8th harmonic eight times in one synodic cycle. Within the 4th harmonic are four aspects. The opposition point is midway through the synodic cycle. When Venus and Mars are opposite each other (*opposing* as we say in astrology), they are at the middle of their synodic cycle. All aspects that occur prior to the mid-point of the synodic cycle are waxing aspects. All aspects that occur after the mid-point of the synodic cycle are waning aspects. Most of us have a pretty clear orientation to this with the Sun and the Moon. The Sun-Moon synodic cycle is approximately 29 days. It begins with the New Moon when the Sun and the Moon conjunct. The Moon grows in size as it pulls away from the Sun, i.e. the waxing moon time. After the Full Moon, the Moon begins to move toward the Sun again and starts to loose its visibility. The Full Moon is when the Sun and the Moon are opposite, aka the mid-point of their synodic cycle. After the mid-point, the Moon is waning.

Waxing aspects are building aspects. Just as the Moon builds in brightness as it is waxing, all planets build in brightness as they are waxing. Waxing aspects are creative, energized. They have force and tend to be driving and pushing us toward something. Waxing aspects require work and ask us to move towards our goals, wishes or dreams. With *applying* waxing aspects, we are challenged to find a new way to either deal with the challenge or honor the gift. With *separating* waxing aspects, the initial challenge has been met and we are asked to move forward with a motion that is already in place.

Waning aspects are reaping aspects. We are benefitting from the work we did during the waxing time, whether that occurred in this lifetime or at some other prior time. Waning aspects are time to coast, ease off intensity, and receive. Waning aspects are also letting go and releasing aspects. Waning trines are gifts that we have established and are releasing no matter how much we are using them. Waning squares are challenges that we have already met and where the dynamic motion of these aspects is to be used toward completion or resolution. With a waning aspect that is *applying*, we are asked to use the energy of the aspect this lifetime, to use it for completion. With a *separating* waning aspect, we experience the gift or challenge as very familiar and one in which the letting go has already begun.

Aspects

Planetary Synodic Cycles

	Mercury						
Venus	144.65 D	Venus					
Earth	115.88 D	587.92 D	Earth				
Mars	100.93 D	333.92 D	779.94 D	Mars			
Jupiter	89.92 D	236.99 D	398.55 D	816.44 D	Jupiter		
Saturn	88.73 D	229.49 D	378.09 D	733.86 D	19.86 Y	Saturn	
Uranus	88.25 D	226.36 D	369.66 D	708.74 D	13.81 Y	45.36 Y	Uranus
Neptune	88.13 D	225.54 D	367.49 D	694.94 D	12.91 Y	35.87 Y	171.40 Y	Pluto
Pluto	88.09 D	225.26 D	366.73 D	693.22 D	12.46 Y	33.42 Y	126.94 Y	489.45 Y

D=Days
Y=Years

Table of Aspects with Definitions

Aspect	Degrees Harmonic	Orb	Description
Conjunction ☌	0° All	10°	The two planets join forces and operate as one. The two planets complement each other and work together for a common purpose. There is added intensity in the area and sign of the two planets. It can be hard to tell the difference between the two planets, as they operate together. It's like the two planets create some kind of hybrid planet that includes all of the traits of both planets. In this case, one plus one equals more than two. The hybrid planet is more powerful than both simply added together. Always, astrologers place significance on two or more planets in conjunction.
Semi-sextile ⚺	30° 12th	1°	This is a very subtle aspect, rarely noticed and rarely used for interpretation. It's like a gentle itch, nudging us to get on with it. **Waxing**: A nudge to grow **Waning**: A nudge to pull inward
Semi-square ∠	45° 8th	2°	Like all of the 8th harmonic aspects, we are challenged to make a change. This aspect suggests a place where we have a hard time adapting, where we stay stuck in old attitudes that we have inherited from previous generations. We may think we know what is going on with a certain air of arrogance, while being completely wrong. The two planets are pointing to an attitude that we need to change, yet are very resistant to changing. It's the habit that all of our friends see, that we keep insisting is helping us, but it isn't. It is getting in the way of our full happiness and joy in life. **Waxing**: The stress of not getting what we want pushes us to change our attitude and open our minds so that we are able to experience more joy **Waning**: The stress of not getting what we want helps us to clear old, negative, inherited thought patterns
Sextile ⚹	60° 6th, 12th	3°	The two planets work together to bring forth a gift and an opportunity. These two planets like each other and support ease and grace in the areas in which they exist. **Waxing**: Curiosity and expression of a talent or place of ease that opens us into new opportunities **Waning**: Expression of a gift that supports opportunities to receive love and abundance

Aspects

Aspect	Degrees Harmonic	Orb	Description
Square □	90° 4th, 8th, 12th	8°	Squares push us to grow. The two planets create the perfect circumstances for us to have to face a part of ourselves that absolutely needs to change this lifetime. There is no way out when two planets square. The two energies must confront each other. This is an aspect of motivation and drive. The challenge creates heat and passion, a need to make the world a better place, a need to make ourselves a better person. The challenges that these two planets reflect in our experience are unavoidable. The square calls for decisive action and a willingness to take risks even if failure is likely. This can be a frustrating aspect if no outlet for the energy is visible. Keep looking, there is always a way through. **Waxing**: Conflict that threatens our sense of security, drive to make a difference in our personal lives **Waning**: Conflict that pushes us to accept responsibility for our action, drive to make a difference in the world
Trine △	120° 3rd, 6th, 9th, 12th	8°	The two planets work together in total harmony. There can be so much harmony that the two planets lay dormant, as if there is no need to express or make a difference. It is the gift that comes so easily that we deny its validity. Without a square or other stressor to trigger the trine, the two planets support ease and comfort. **Waxing**: Creative expression, gifts expressed with a desire for recognition **Waning**: Gifts expressed with a desire to make a difference
Sesqui-quadrate	135° 8th	2°	The two planets in sesquiquadrate are duking it out for a place in full light, the planets are either moving toward or away from the opposition. The challenge is to make changes so that we accept our destiny, our calling in life. We are challenged to take steps toward our dreams. The two planets are pushing us to step it up, get focused and use any experience of frustration to be more disciplined. The stressors that come with this aspect push us to set goals and take action. **Waxing**: Moving forward with life goals **Waning**: Adjusting our goals to be in alignment with supporting others

Aspect	Degrees Harmonic	Orb	Description
Quincunx ⚻	150° 12th	1°	This is the therapy aspect. The two planets are not in direct conflict, but they don't get along. They aren't in the same element or modality, so there is no direct challenge or harmony. The two planets are adjusting to each other, trying to find a way to coexist. This is an aspect of doing inner work, finding the stillness within. **Waxing**: The health quincunx, the work is to use our mind to re-organize patterns in our body **Waning**: The death quincunx, psychological and emotional adjustment is needed to cope with necessary loss
Opposition ☍	180° 2nd, 4th, 6th, 8th, 10th, 12th	10°	The two planets are showing each other what needs to change in order to function more fully with grace and ease. There is pressure for some movement to occur. Often the two planets operate in some kind of extreme until a balance between the two is found. This is a stressful aspect until we find each planet's unique expression and can be in that while still paying attention to the opposing planet. **Waxing**: The pressure is to grow and express fully **Waning**: The pressure is to get over it and on with it
Quintile **Q**	72° 5th, 10th	4°	The two planets in this aspect want to grow organically, in harmony with nature, but first there needs to be in attunement with nature. The quintile supports creativity and enhanced relationships. This is the magician's aspect, the chemist's aspect, and the scientist's aspect. It supports creative intelligence and genius that is beneficial and integrated. The gifts of this aspect can be assimilated into productive support to others and the world. Musical and artistic abilities are often indicated. **Waxing**: The creative expression advances one's standing in the world **Waning**: The growth moves one toward resolution and completion
Bi-quintile Q^2	144° 5th, 10th	4°	Like the quintile, this is an aspect of alchemy and magic, the ability to grow and perform. The creativity of this aspect presents itself with passion. There is an added desire to perform and entertain. **Waxing**: Creativity and passion open doorways for performance **Waning**: Creativity and passion support accomplishment and mastery

Aspects

Aspect	Degrees Harmonic	Orb	Description
Septile **S**	51 1/2° 7th	2°	The septile is the mystical and strange tendencies of things descending from other realms, vision, transfiguration, dissolving of boundaries and the propensity to transcend ordinary reality. **Waxing**: Initiation **Waning**: Transcendence
Bi-septile S^2	103° 7th	2°	The bi-septile, like the septile, has an element of the strange and sometimes deceptive quality of otherworldliness. The longing to fit in may be stronger and less likely to be fulfilled. In some way, this aspect sets us apart from others. **Waxing**: Integration of purpose of creative aspect **Waning**: Integration of process which has begun and is called to completion
Tri-septile S^3	154 1/2° 7th	2°	Like the septile, our genius does not fit in to the world and we have to balance our personal needs with the uniqueness of our calling. **Waxing**: Adjustment needed for fulfillment of process and purpose **Waning**: A deeply reflective aspect, calling for spiritual practice and objective witnessing
Novile **N**	40° 9th	1°	The novile, the ninth harmonic, is one of completion and fulfillment. The higher the number of the harmonic, the subtler the experience of the aspect is. By the ninth harmonic, the experience of the aspect is only noticeable if we are on a spiritual path and have a well-developed sense of the unseen realms. In Vedic astrology, the ninth harmonic chart, the Navamsa, is an important chart showing the partner, but also and perhaps more importantly it shows what bears fruit in the individual's life. We look to the ninth harmonic for that which ripens and culminates this lifetime. **Waxing**: What needs to be completed is introduced **Waning**: The completion of the completion

Aspect	Degrees Harmonic	Orb	Description
Bi-novile N²	80° 9th	1°	The mystical aspect of the novile is more present in the bi-novile. As the bi-novile introduces the square that comes in at 90 degrees, there is more of a stress to complete, more pressure for the soul gifts to bear fruit. **Waxing**: Testing of the karmic ground, longing for an end **Waning**: One last push before completion
Tri-novile (Trine) N³	120° 9th	1°	*See the Trine* **Waxing**: The karmic ground covered is available as a strength for moving forward with one's purpose **Waning**: The karmic resolution and availability of a gift to be used for the world
Quart-novile N⁴	160° 9th	1°	The quart-novile has more pressure and stress to move our compassion into a path of service than the novile. The devotion in the novile wants to be shared with others. **Waxing**: Moving into the turning point of an important resolution of karma **Waning**: Moving into the last part of the karmic cycle of resolution, letting go
Decile D	36° 10th	1°	The decile brings celebration, creation, magic, joy, and deliverance. The five meets its match, its mirror. This aspect supports the planets involved to do magic both for manifestation and for ascension. The fulfillment of heaven on earth and earth in heaven.
Tri-Decile D³	108° 10th	1°	*Same as the decile.*
Undecile U	32.73° 11th	1°	All undeciles are about the intention to ascend and find higher ground, a larger perspective which increases our consciousness and serves to create peace and the spread of love throughout this realm
Thirteenths	27.7° 13th	.5°	The aspect which helps us to tune into wisdom and experience of those resonances that are beyond what we can detect with ordinary measures and in ordinary time
Quindecile	165° 24th	.5°	A stress which offers the opportunity to let go and learn through separation and through overcoming obstacles

Finding Aspects in a Chart

Every thirty degrees of the zodiac is equal to one sign. At first, actually count the number of degrees between two planets. One trick: a ninety-degree aspect (a square) will be equal to three signs difference. You can count the signs that are shown on the cusps and interceptions of the signs. A common beginner error is to count houses. The number of houses between two planets in a particular aspect can vary. Again, count the number of degrees or signs—not the number of houses.

A better way to easily find aspects, especially squares and trines, is to memorize signs in the same element and the same modality. Remember that the elements are *Fire* (Aries, Leo and Sagittarius), *Earth* (Taurus, Virgo and Capricorn), *Air* (Gemini, Libra and Aquarius) and *Water* (Cancer, Scorpio and Pisces). The modalities are *Cardinal* (Aries, Cancer, Libra and Capricorn), *Fixed* (Taurus, Leo, Scorpio and Aquarius) and *Mutable* (Gemini, Virgo, Sagittarius and Pisces).

Trines (120°) will correspond to planets in the same element. Squares (90°) will correspond to planets in the same modality. Occasionally, you will encounter what we call **disassociated aspects**, where the two planets are on the cusp and one is in one element or modality and the other planet is in a sign of a different element or modality.

Example: Venus is at 29° Aries and Mars is at 01° Leo. These two planets are actually 92° apart which is a square. However, they are in the same element (fire, in this case). This is a *disassociated* square. Basically, it is still a square but is somewhat weakened in its effect.

Another example: Mercury is at 28° Taurus and Saturn is at 02° Libra. These two planets are 124° apart—which is within orb for a trine. However, the planets are not in signs that are in the same element. This is a disassociated trine and is a somewhat weaker trine than if both planets are in signs of the same element. Any and all aspects can be disassociated.

How to determine waxing and waning:

Here is the trick that I have discovered to be the easiest. Take the slower moving planet and rotate the chart until that planet looks like it is at nine o'clock on the chart; i.e. the ascendant. Then look at the faster moving planet in the aspect. If the faster moving planet is in the bottom half of the chart, that aspect is waxing. If the faster moving planet is in the top half of the chart, that aspect is waning. Remember that the planets move clockwise through the houses, unless they are moving retrograde. The Nodes of the Moon naturally move retrograde.

For all intents and purposes, the speed of the planets goes in this order from slowest to fastest:

Pluto
Neptune
Uranus
Chiron
Saturn
Jupiter
Many of the asteroids
Mars
Sun/Earth
Venus
Mercury
Moon
Ascendant

While the actual speeds of the planets remain constant, the apparent speeds from our vantage point of Earth do vary. Sometimes, Neptune appears to move slower than Pluto. Sometimes Chiron appears to move faster than Saturn. When Mars or Venus stations, they appear to be standing still and are therefore moving slower than any of the others. In general, this order will give you what you need to determine relative speeds.

Multiple Aspect Patterns

As this is an overview workbook and a basic introduction to astrology, I will provide a cursory glance into some of the more significant aspect patterns that occur when more than two planets are aspecting each other. This is an important part of interpreting a chart and requires more study than I will give it room for here. Bil Tierney's book, *Dynamics of Aspect Analysis,* is a classic I recommend for delving into these aspect patterns.

T-Square	When two or more planets are in opposition and a third planet is squaring the opposing planet.	A common aspect pattern that supports us in being driven and motivated. The stress placed on the squaring planet pushes us to make something of ourselves in the world.
Grand Square	Four (or more) planets squaring each other, such that all four corners of the square are filled. There are two oppositions in a Grand Square.	This is an aspect pattern of ambition and drive, of power and a stress. We may feel like we have some particular destiny this lifetime that must be fulfilled that lights a fire under us until we know we are on track toward fulfillment.
Grand Trine	Three or more planets trining each other, forming three points of an equilateral triangle.	The three planets will all be in the same element and three different modalities. This is an aspect pattern that displays great talents and gifts, something we come into this life knowing well. This is a pattern of ease and sometimes laziness.
Yod	Two planets sextile, while a third planet quincunxes both of them forming a bi-lateral triangle.	This is an aspect pattern of destiny. The quincunxing planet is called the apex planet and it points to a particular path that we must resolve this lifetime. The point opposite the apex planet is the reaction point. Transits to the reaction point signify times when the Yod is activated. Those times are chances to fulfill our destiny.
Grand Sextile	Six planets all sextiling each other, forming a six-sided figure. Two Grand Trines opposing each other.	The two Grand Trines activate each other, awakening our gifts and offering opportunities for expression. Grand Sextiles signify people who are comfortable being on this planet and feel like they have been here many times. They are usually comfortable in nature and have a deep connection to Mother Earth.

Table of Aspects in Order of Degrees

Symbol	Degrees	Aspect	Orb	Harmonic
☌	0°	Conjunct	10°	1
	27.7°	Thirteenth	.5°	13
⚺	30°	Semi-sextile	1°	12
	32.7	Undecile	1°	11
D	36°	Decile	1°	10
N	40°	Novile	1°	9
∠	45°	Semi-square	2°	8
S	51.5°	Septile	2°	7
	55.4°	Thirteenth	.5°	13
⚹	60°	Sextile	3°	6
	65.5°	Undecile	1°	11
Q	72°	Quintile	4°	5
N²	80°	Bi-novile	1°	9
	83.1°	Thirteenth	.5°	13
□	90°	Square	8°	4
	98.2°	Undecile	1°	11
S²	103°	Bi-septile	2°	7
D³	108°	Tri-decile	1°	10
	110.1°	Thirteenth	.5°	13
△	120°	Trine	8°	3
⚼	135°	Sesquiquadrate	2°	8
	138.5°	Thirteenth	.5°	13
Q²	144°	Bi-quintile	4°	5
⚻	150°	Quincunx	1°	12
S³	154.5°	Tri-septile	2°	7
N⁴	160°	Quart-novile	1°	9
	165°	Quindecile	.5°	24
	166.2°	Thirteenth	.5°	13
☍	180°	Opposition	10°	2

Exercise: Aspects

Use the blank wheel on the next page and draw in your chart. Pay attention to each symbol you draw. Figure out your aspects and with colored pencils, draw lines connecting the two planets that are in aspect to each other.

The colors I typically use are:

yellow = opposition
red = square
orange = inconjunct
green = trine
blue = sextile
dark blue = quintile
purple = septiles
pink = quincunx

In the empty boxes, write in the aspect between the two planets. For extra credit figure out the orbs as well.

	☉	☽	☿	♀	♂	♃	♄	♅	♆	♇
☉										
☽										
☿										
♀										
♂										
♃										
♄										
♅										
♆										
♇										

Aspects

Aspects

General Guidelines for Interpreting & Integrating Aspects

1. Consider **the meaning of the aspect**. Conjunctions are unification and focus. Oppositions are a search for balance. Squares are highest degree of interaction. Trines are strength. Sextiles are opportunities. Inconjuncts are stressors needing resolution. etc.

2. Consider **the meanings of the planets** involved.

3. Consider **other aspects to the planets involved**. These are influences that support or challenge the aspect. Other aspects can offer information for how to deal with the aspect at hand.

4. Consider **the signs the planets are in.**
Make special note of the **elements** and **modalities** involved.

5. Consider **the houses of the planets** involved.

6. Consider **the planets dispositing** the planets in the aspect.
(A dispositor is the planet that rules the sign that the planet is in.)

7. Consider **the overall aspect pattern** of which this aspect is a part.

The Phases of the Moon

The phase of the Moon when we are born is very important to understanding the entire chart. The Moon reflects the Sun's light. It offers us an understanding and perspective on who we are (the Sun). The Moon shows us ourselves back to ourselves. It represents our ability to process the experiences we have in life. The Moon speaks to how supported we feel in life. In Vedic astrology, it is more important than the Sun, as the Sun represents our ego, who we identify ourselves to be, while the Moon taps us into cosmic consciousness. It is the Moon that wakes up the Divine within and shares that divinity with the world.

The relationship between the Moon and the Sun tells us how well we know ourselves. The brighter the Moon, the more aware we are of our ego attachments (Sun). The Moon offers us an ability to see our foibles and strengths, our pains and passions. When the Moon is darker, we may feel like we are more in the dark with who we are. We may find our very identity a mystery. Many highly conscious people were born during a dark moon, but they may find that what they are doing on this planet at this time is a bit more of a mystery to themselves. Others can see their talents and challenges more than they can see them themselves.

To figure out what Moon phase you were born in, start by looking at the Sun in your chart. Take the Sun as a fixed point. Since the Moon moves faster than the Sun, note whether the Moon is moving away from or toward the Sun. If the Moon is moving away from the Sun, it is waxing. If the Moon is moving toward the Sun, it is completing it's journey in relationship to the Sun, aka waning. Next calculate how many degrees apart the Moon is from the Sun.

New Moon 0° to 45° waxing

This begins the synodic cycle of the Sun and Moon. The Moon is dark and building. During this lifetime, we will be learning through taking chances. We will be open to trying on new things. We will likely be finding our way through doing many different things. Since we are at the beginning of a new cycle, we aren't quite sure who we are. Life is an adventure with many opportunities and possibilites. Our exploits and explorations may occur as slightly random. The world offers us a wide range of events to learn from.

Crescent Moon 45° to 90° waxing

During the Crescent phase we know a bit more about ourselves. We are testing our theories about life and pushing ourselves to be better. We are beginning to work toward goals and explore with focus. We are learning about making choices and the need to use our will force to explore our very personal and unique nature. The challenges in life show up to teach us discernment, which may be difficult at this stage.

The Phases of the Moon

First Quarter Moon 90° to 135° waxing

When we are born during the First Quarter phase, we know we were born with a purpose and we are dared by the world to find it. We are challenged to explore who we really are. We often have a sense of determination to find our purpose when we are born during this moon phase. We are growing and learning about ourselves with lessons that come rapidly. We often have drive and ambition. There is sometimes a sense of urgency about our purpose, like there is in a twenty-five year old. The world is our oyster, if only the world would get out of our way and let us get on with it. We can feel frustration at the setbacks. Usually the setbacks are there to help us get on the right track. It is easy to get off-track with this Moon phase, and boldly go in the wrong direction. However, being off-track is part of being on-track with this First Quarter Moon. Once we recognize that a course correction is needed, we usually have the courage and determination to do it all better the next time.

Gibbous Moon 135° to 180° waxing

Gibbous Moons rarely get the respect they deserve. During this stage, we are learning to take one step back and two steps forward. Sometimes there is a drive to head to the finish line, a feeling like there is something we have to do and it's important. While we are seeing the big picture, we feel a need to pursue our goals with focused intent. We are aligning attention and intention with full light shining on our dreams and soul work. In Vedic astrology, this is the most auspicious Moon phase, because the Moon is both bright and growing, especially the closer to Full it is.

Full Moon 180° to 225° (135° to 180° waning)

The bright Moon sheds full light on our path. We know who we are and we are hell-bent on showing the world what we are made of. We find we are important and seen in the fields in which we work and play. We often feel supported in unique ways by random strangers. Being able to see, we can offer our insights and perspective to the world in ways that others can receive. Since the Moon is waning during this phase, there can be a deeper inner relaxation and/or a desire to move into greater ease, at least more than the prior cycles.

Inclined Moon 225° to 270° (90° to 135° waning)

When we are born during the Inclined Moon, we are working to integrate the lessons of life while at this same time working toward accomplishment. We have drive and ambition, but long to use this for only one or two things, as if those few things had the utmost of weight attached to them. We know who we are but are beginning to lose sight of it. This growth process is teaching us to trust that those around us support us. Better yet, we are learning that even when it seems that no one has our back, the Universe in its perfection and divine order offer us the perfect support. We are learning to receive and see the support that comes to us especially when it comes in a way that we were not expecting.

Last Quarter Moon 270° to 315° (45° to 90° waning)

Those of us born during the Last Quarter Moon are learning to release attachment. We have an inner wisdom that comes through just when we need it most. As we move through our lives, the experiences we have teach us more about who we have become rather than who we might be. We are healing past lives and working through ancestral patterns. Our performances may be skilled and many things come easy to us. At the same time, we may long intensely for something that continually eludes us. As soon as we let it go, there it is. We may find that we are finishing up other people's unfinished business. It seems to work best if we simply own it as our own and get on with it.

Balsamic Moon 315° to 360° (0° to 45° waning)

You are the magic makers in the world. You are here to work in the mystery. You are finding the gems of life in the moments when everyone else is lost. While you might feel lost yourselves, you are concluding a Lunar Synodic cycle and bridging this life with other lives. You tend to be creative as you are comfortable being in the unknown, at least more comfortable than most people. Your inability to see who you really are comes with humility and compassion. You are the guides for others as they work to find what you know intuitively.

Exercise: Phases of the Moon

From looking at your chart, figure out your moon phase. Start at the Sun and count the degrees going counter-clockwise until you reach the Moon. Journal about how your Moon phase mirrors your life. Consider how bright your Moon is and how this reflects on your experience. Also note if you were born during the day or night. If you were born during the day, the Sun becomes a more predominant force. If you were born at night, the Moon takes on more significance. Note if both Sun and Moon are out (above the horizon) or are invisible (below the horizon) or if one is out and other invisible. Consider what the sky looked like when you were born.

Paying attention to the Lunar Phases has a long history. For a month, pay attention to the Moon. Go out and look at it each night or day. Follow the Moon phases and do rituals for the New and Full Moons. New Moon rituals are supportive for beginnings and setting intentions. Full Moon rituals are good to do with other people in bringing things to light, celebrating and acknowledging our gifts and/or challenges, and transforming situations in our lives in which we would like to see change. Also, honor the Balsamic Moon time for clearing and cleaning.

Declinations

Declination is a term used to describe the number of degrees north or south of the equatorial plane a planet is. The equatorial plane is the projection of the plane coming out of the equator of Earth, as if the equator represents a disk that extended past the Earth's crust into space.

When two planets are the same number of degrees of declination and both are either North or South, then we say they are parallel. These two planets will operate in a similar way as if they were conjunct.

When two planets are the same number of degrees and in opposite directions, i.e. one is North and the other is South, they are contra-parallel. They will operate as if they are in opposition.

When two planets are both parallel and conjunct, they are eclipsed and this is very powerful to note. The conjunction is much strengthened by this and the eclipse can overshadow the chart. Same goes if two planets are in opposition and contra-parallel. I noticed during a powerful 6.8 earthquake, in my hometown of Olympia, a Mercury-Uranus eclipse was occurring.

The declinations can be found in some ephemerides and most computer programs. Typically a 1-degree orb is used but I have seen as wide as a 2-degree-34' orb used successfully.

Exercise: Declinations

Find the parallels and contra-parallels in your chart. You will need to get this information from a separate chart. How do the two or more planets operate together?

Find if you have any eclipses. Note if the eclipses and parallels and contra-parallels play any part in a major aspect pattern.

How does the eclipse/parallel or contra-parallel intensify a dynamic in your chart?

Look at any transits to the planets that are parallel or contra-parallel. Does it change your interpretation of those planets?

Transits

Take any moment in time and relate it to any other moment in time and you have a transit. In astrology, we look at the patterns of one moment in time and draw correlations with another moment, studying the geometric relationship between the two. Transits are the interplay of cycles upon cycles. It is one planet witnessing itself, witnessing another planet or witnessing another place in the wheel. A natal chart freezes a moment in time and space. The natal chart shows us the energetic patterns that hold the imprints of the heavens upon a soul. Transits bring that moment into the present moment, or into any other moment. Transits awaken the soul through ringing our vibrational bell.

Transits are the planets in the sky aspecting a planet or planets in another chart, as in a natal chart. Transits are one of the most important ways in which timing of events is predicted and understood. Use the Ephemeris to look back into your life at major turning points. Notice which planets were aspecting your natal chart. You can learn a lot about how you personally deal with certain transits by looking back in your life.

When planets in the sky form a pattern of energy that coincides with our chart, it resonates in our chart. The waves of energy, the vibrations, from the patterns in the sky, resonate with our birth pattern—the one we carry with us throughout our lives. So the transits are awakening, enlivening, vibrating in tune with our own resonant system. They wake us up to our pattern. How they do this depends on the nature of the planet itself, the sign it is in, the angle it is making and our natal pattern.

When looking at transits, first notice what planets in the sky are conjunct planets in your natal chart. Then look at the drama and the role that that planet plays in your natal chart. Then look at how that will be activated by the transiting planet. Then look at transiting planets that are opposing natal planets, then look to squares, then trines, then sextiles and on and on.

Example: Someone has natal Mars at 24° Taurus and Saturn in the sky is at 24° Taurus-conjunct natal Mars. What is Mars' role in the natal dynamic? Well, let us say the Mars is in a Grand Trine with Jupiter and Mercury. This is an Earth Grand Trine. These are about gifts on the material plane—being able to think concretely, realistically and clearly (Mercury), believing that anything is possible on the physical plane (Jupiter) and being able to act on both the thought and belief (Mars). Not a bad thing to have in a natal chart.

Saturn is the planet of bringing things into form, lessons and grounding. When Saturn crosses the Mars point in the trine, it teaches that sometimes we have to wait for things to take shape, must work hard for things to happen and yet it also offers the opportunity for the gift of the Grand Trine to be made manifest. Depending on how this person has dealt with this trine will determine how Saturn impacts them. If this person has struggled to even know that this gift exists, Saturn may offer a hard lesson for them to find out. If the person has been accessing this trine and has achieved a certain success in their life then Saturn may come as a boon to support a long-term project or dream in coming into form.

A note on Resonance:

Resonance is a well recorded and little understood phenomena of physics. A note played on the piano that is the same frequency as a guitar string will cause that nearby guitar string to ring. A radio picks up sound waves tuned to a certain frequency. Resonance is the interaction of a wave with another wave — both waves being the same frequency or a harmonic frequency.

"Resonance is when you have two bodies that oscillate at the same natural speed — then they are in resonance with each other. Where you have two separate bodies — resonant bodies — that are moving at the same speed with each other, then you can induce one to move the other. That is in resonance. They transfer energy. When you are in resonance you can transfer energy from one to the other".[9] Dan Dial

When someone says something to us that "rings" true, we might say that that resonates. This is physically happening, since thoughts and words have a wave form and a frequency. Since they are a waveform with a frequency and we each have a natural frequency, a thought can resonate with our frequency. It may not be true for someone else with a different frequency. Or it may be a core truth that is at a frequency that all humans vibrate to in some form. When we are in resonance with a thought or with another person or thing, we are actually transferring energy.

---

[9] My conversations with Dan Dial took place in Shelton, Washington between October 1999 and July 2001. Our sessions were recorded and transcribed. The quotes are direct quotes from these sessions. I spent many, many hours studying and relistening to the teachings that Dan Dial generously offered me during this time. It took me years to understand some of the most basic principles. I live in deep appreciation for the transmission of these teachings and for the work of Dan and his open-hearted wife, Landi Dial.

The Ephemeris

The Ephemeris is the astrologer's most important book. It is a book of tables that contain the coordinates of the planets on any given day. For each day of the month, you can look at this book and tell where each planet is—the sign and approximate number of degrees. The Moon moves quickly and must be calculated for true accuracy. Most ephemeride tables are done at Greenwich Mean Time (GMT). Some ephemerides will be calculated for Noon GMT and some for Midnight GMT. Therefore the degrees will be slightly off of the actual degrees. However, this is the book that is used to calculate with precision your natal chart and any other chart.

This is an important book to become familiar with. Look at it. Notice how quickly or slowly each planet moves. Look at how often they go retrograde and direct.[10] Retrograde is noted by an R. If the planet is retrograde for the entire month, the R shows up at the top of the column. D stands for direct and is noted when the planet changes from retrograde to direct. Otherwise, it is assumed that the planet is moving direct.

Another thing that most ephemerides have is a clue as to when the eclipses occur. In Michelson's *The American Ephemeris for the 21st Century*, eclipse data is found at the bottom in a box. The symbols that denote eclipses are the conjunction or opposition sign filled in. Eclipses occur when the Sun, Moon and Earth are in direct alignment. Solar Eclipses occur at New Moons while Lunar Eclipses occur at Full Moons.

In the Neil F. Michelsen ephemeris, there is an excellent page of explanation at the very beginning of the book. I recommend you read this page. I just did for the first time and found it to be very helpful.

---

[10] Michelsen, Neil. (revisions by Pottenger, Rique). *The American Ephemeris for the 21st Century: 2000 to 2050 at Midnight, Expanded Second Edition.* San Diego, CA: ACS Publications, 1982; 1997.

Progressions

Progressions are a way of moving a chart forward based on different time patterns. There are a number of ways to progress a natal chart. The Naibod Secondary Progressed Chart is the most commonly used. In this chart, every year of the native's life is equal to a day in the life of the planets—a day-for-a-year. A person who is thirty years old would look to the placement of the planets thirty days after they were born.[11] Other progressions used are a day-for-a-month and a month-for-a-year. Solar Arc Direction, usually lumped in with progressions, is another similar tool. Its calculation is based on the arc of the Sun. The Sun moves about a degree every day. In the Solar Arc Direction, every planet is progressed by the same number of degrees as the secondary progressed Sun. So if you are forty-five years old, every planet is moved 45 degrees from its natal position. In this way, the aspects all remain the same. Each progression is used for a different purpose.

Naibod Secondary Progression

Our life appears to be a linear progression of events over a period we call years. Experiences happen in those years and alter the way we interact with life and the way we perceive reality. It is easy to think of the movement of the planets in real-time affecting us—the transits. But if we are able to perceive reality at a different harmonic, then we might see the progressed planets as affecting us as well.

Take this to the level of interpretation.
The transits show us what we are learning about ourselves in "real" time. They show us how we are able to alter our life as we know it with all of the experiences we have garnered in our life. The progressions then show us what we are learning *despite* all of the experiences we have had in this life. It shows us how we can alter our life without all the collection of "stuff" that has clung to us in this life. With this understanding, the progressed chart becomes a tool for looking at what is possible for us to change, to learn, to be, regardless of the tapes we collected from childhood, regardless of that bad experience we had in the 8th grade that we continue to recreate, regardless of the titles we give ourselves, etc. We can use the progressed chart to look at who we have become in the meantime. And we can use the progressed chart to look at where in our life we can make significant change without this lifetime's collection of tapes.

There are two ways the secondary progressed chart is used.
1. As a whole chart reflecting our current state of evolution. We look at the chart as if it were a natal chart, a more current natal chart that reflects who we have become. It shows us who we have grown into. It shows us who we are now.
2. As a transit chart interacting with our natal chart. We use the planets in the secondary progressed chart as if they were transiting our natal chart.

---

[11] See Appendix A for an explanation of why the Progressed chart works.

Way 1: As an updated natal chart

Use everything we have learned so far and apply it to your secondary progressed chart. Find your new Sun sign, Moon sign and other planets. What house are they in now? Since the Sun changes signs roughly every thirty days, our progressed Sun changes signs every thirty years. So if you don't like your Sun sign, you do get a new one every thirty years. ;) The Moon sign will change about every two and half years. Most of us will have changes in our Mercury, Venus, and Mars signs as well. The slower planets may also change within our lifetime.

Besides looking at your new Sun and Moon signs, also note the phase of the Moon in the progressed chart. The outer planets will be pretty close to the same place as when you were born, being that they move so slowly. However, the older you are the bigger the difference between your natal and your progressed chart.

Way 2: As transit chart

Part of the reason I think that astrologers love the progressed chart is that we get to have prolonged Venus transits. Using the progressed chart as a transit chart, the inner planets become the significant players. The outer planets move too slow to matter, but Mars can transit a significant place in our natal chart for five years and produce significant changes.

Progressed Sun transit: Sheds a splotlight on the planet it is transitting, offering a vital period, with the potential for increased health, joy and self-esteem.
Progressed Moon transit: Wakes us up to the truth of the issues that the transitted planet offers us. We can open our perspective to see our issues with greater clarity. There is a chance for healing and recovery.
Progressed Mercury transit: Helps us understand and communicate our understandings with greater clarity. Mercury can offer us increased capacity to make wise decisions.
Progressed Venus transit: Offers us a chance for love. Relationships take on greater importance. Venus can also support increased abundance and creativity.
Progressed Mars transit: Supports us in taking action. We can be spurred on to initiate change. We may feel more courage. The planet that is being transitted can be more energized. The challenges of that planet may also be triggered into greater intensity at this time, offering us a chance to make deep and lasting changes.
Progressed Jupiter transit: Expands our worldview so that we see the patterns of this planet with new eyes. We may have more opportunities and find more doors open to us.
Progressed Saturn transit: Focuses our attention on the issues of the planet. We have to work through challenges that support us in completing significant past life karma. Saturn moves very slowly in the progressed chart, so it is unlikely that you will have a progressed transit of Saturn that isn't already happening in your natal chart.

Important Progressed Transits to Note

1. **Progressed Venus conjunct the Sun or Progressed Sun conjunct Venus.**

We all get one of these within the first sixty years of life. I use a one-degree orb, so the transit will last around two years. It is one of the most accurate predictors for meeting a life mate. However, other factors need to be at play. By itself, this transit will not bring love. Yet, it almost always supports us in opening to more love in our life. I look at it as a doorway into the potential for true love. Once we move through the door, we are on the other side and are more available to having a true heart-opening experience of love. Sometimes this happens when we are a baby. I have observed that people who have this transit as a child more easily move into relationships and are more likely to meet a life partner and be happy in love.

2. **Any planet changing direction in our progressed chart.**

If we are born with a planet retrograde, we are often out of step with society when it comes to the themes of that planet. When the planet changes direction and goes direct, we may find that we are more in tuned with society when it comes to the themes of that planet. As the planet stations, notice any planets that it is transiting in the natal chart. That planet will become very important.

Mercury: People born with Mercury retrograde tend to be more intuitive and creative. Sometimes they are slow to speak or write and may have some learning challenges. At the same time, they are often unusually gifted in some other way. When Mercury goes direct by progression in their lifetime, then they may find they can communicate with greater ease. If you are born with Mercury direct and it goes retrograde, you may find yourself moving into a 21-year creative time.

Venus: People born with Venus retrograde tend to bring in extra relationship baggage from past lives. They are often working out issues of self-love. Many times they have experienced abandonment in childhood. When Venus stations and goes direct, they are offered a chance to complete the past life karma that may have been plaguing them since childhood. In this case, there often comes a time when progressed Venus transits natal Venus. This becomes a very important time for beginning or deepening into a significant relationship. Venus retrogrades last forty days and therefore a progressed Venus time will last forty years.

Mars: People born with Mars retrograde are often ancient warriors healing their battle wounds from past lives. Sometimes there is trauma in childhood that reflects these old battle wounds. When Mars stations and goes direct, the native may find they are healed from some old wound, either physical or emotional. If Mars stations and goes retrograde by progression, we may move into a more internal or reflective period of time. Since Mars goes retrograde for about 66 days, a progressed Mars retrograde period can last for 66 years, thus usually making it a once in a lifetime shift.

3. **Lunar Phase change.**

Note the phase of the Moon in your progressed chart. When your progressed chart is a New Moon, it initiates the beginning of a thirty-year cycle. This is very significant. Any planets that are conjunct, opposite or square the progressed New Moon will be important planets for the following 30 years. If Venus is conjunct the progressed New Moon, it will begin a thirty-year period that will be good for love and wealth. We can break this thirty-year cycle into four sections of about seven years. When we are in the first quarter phase, the Moon squares the Sun, and that begins a seven-year time period. Any planets conjunct or opposite the Sun or Moon in that chart will also be very significant. Also note the Full Moon and the waning square (last quarter moon) for the other seven-year time periods.

Example: If Saturn is moving retrograde when a person is born, they are typically out of step with the culture. The retrograde motion at birth is also significant of past life lessons carried into this lifetime (especially Saturn). The nature of the lessons would correspond to the sign, house and aspects to Saturn. Once we have looked at the karmic condition, we can look at the progressed chart to see at what age the person can look forward to completing that round of lessons. There are two dates to look at: 1) the date the planet moves direct and 2) the date the planet conjuncts itself. In the case of Saturn, it is rare to have both dates in one lifetime, but it is possible.

All of this takes me to the age-old question of fate and free will. The progressed chart has an element of fate in it. A planet shifts direction and the past life lesson is complete whether we do anything about it or not. At the same time, how we experience life seems to be a function of what we intend and our clarity that is a function of what we have done with the opportunities the stars and life offer us. Both are occurring at the same time.

Postscript

Astrology is a powerful tool for helping us tap into Universal wisdom. Recently, a young astrologer brought up the issue that scientists have come to call the Heisenberg principle — the observer affects the observed. Yes, as soon as we look at a chart we bring ourselves to the process. At the same time, from my experience, the Universe is more intelligent than I can imagine. Through astrology I get a glimpse of this vast brilliance.

I work with the principle of threes, when I look at a chart. I need to see something three times in the chart before I share the information. Once I hit three times with the chart saying the same thing, I have found a magic synchronicity portal. The idea in a reading is to find as many of these portals as I can find. The more portals I find the more fluid the reading becomes. Information starts to pour forth from some deep well.

Knowing the basic tenets and studying astrology is important, but so is opening up our intuitive channels. To truly understand astrology, we must open up other ways of knowing. There is much that we can deduce through the chart with our logical minds. However, I have found that the gold nuggets are revealed when I can clear my personal issues and open my mind to something beyond logic. Logic is the first step. We have to know what we are looking at. Being a clear channel for truth takes practice and a willingness to let go of control. We have to practice this in our daily lives.

For me, practicing astrology is a path. At this writing, I have been studying for twenty years and almost every day I learn something new. After seventeen years of being a professional western astrologer, I took the dive into Vedic astrology. For the past four years, I have been richly rewarded for this dive. It has added new dimensions to my readings. I think, though, that I needed those seventeen years of practice at a level that I could personally integrate on a daily basis.

Being an astrologer is a great privilege. For me, it is the top of the ladder. I get to hear peoples' stories of truth and depth in a short time. I get to witness their joy and pain and offer a perspective that is bigger than most other perspectives that are available on the planet at this time.

I encourage you to dive into this study with respect and care. Remember to see something three times before you accept it as truth. I have seen many contradictions in charts. A contradiction is an invitation to dive deeper, to ask different questions and to probe further. In the end, the chart is always a clue to the truth of our essence.

Appendix A: How Astrology Works & Why: A Different Perspective

While there can be no denying the moon's influence, critics of astrology argue that the planets are too distant and their forces too weak to affect humanity. But the ability of weak signals to produce substantial effects is well known in physics as the phenomenon of resonance, in which a receiver vibrates to specific frequencies transmitted. Resonance is the cornerstone of the theory of astrological influence propounded by Dr. Percy Seymour, author of *Astrology: The Evidence of Science*. Dr. Seymour believes that the gravity of the moon and planets cause the 'tides' in the earth's magnetosphere. These tides produce electric currents that alter the earth's magnetic field in a regularly repeating pattern. Because the planets move around the sky at different rates, there are distinct frequencies associated with each planet. Certain neural circuits in the human brain can resonate with these frequencies. "All the calculations used by scientists to show that cosmic forces are too weak to affect life on earth have ignored the possibility of resonance. I have used the mathematics of resonance to construct my theory. I am suggesting that a fetus with a given set of inherited characteristics has a nervous system genetically tuned to receiving specific fluctuations of the geomagnetic field, and that it will not respond to others of greater strength to which it is not tuned . . ."[12] This work of Dr. Seymour's aligns directly with my studies with Dan Dial.

After years of studying the work of Nikola Tesla and doing his own high energy experimentation, Dan Dial has come to an understanding of how the universe functions, an understanding that he has applied to his various inventions. His theory resonates for me very deeply and makes sense with all that I have studied both in science and spirituality. Here is a small section that pertains to astrology.

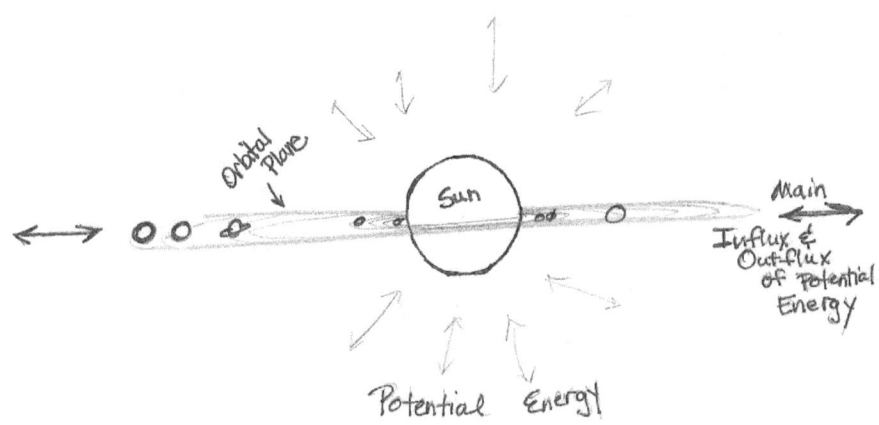

---

[12] Seymour, P.A.H. *Astrology: The Evidence of Science* (revised and extended paperback version), Great Britain: Arkana-Penguin, 1990.

Since potential energy is bombarding this planet all of the time from all over the Universe, the Sun, Moon and all of the planets *block or filter* a small part of this energy as it moves through them and reaches the Earth.

The main influx of potential energy occurs along the orbital plane of the Sun; the plane in which all of the planets reside (yes, all of the planets are in the same plane). The reason that this is the main influx and outflux of energy is due to the fact that it is a plane that is ninety degrees to the plane of the galaxy. According to the laws of magnetics and manifestation, right angles (ninety degrees) are where the greatest amount of energy interchange occurs. Thus, the greatest amount of energy interchange occurs at ninety degrees to the plane of the galaxy (yes, all the stars in the galaxy are roughly in the same plane). Our solar system is a plane that is perpendicular to the plane of the galaxy. This is no coincidence.

The Sun and Moon create the most obvious effects of filtering or changing this energy. They are the largest and the closest to Earth, respectively. When we look at the sky, the Sun and Moon are significantly larger than any of the other planets that look like little stars in the sky. Thus, in astrology, the Sun and Moon are weighted more heavily, as having more significance than the other planets.

We notice the effect of the Moon by the tides. The Moon most intensely filters the energy during a full moon when the Moon is in direct line with the energy from the Universe before it reaches Earth and as it is pulled into the Sun. When this occurs the density of the planet decreases in alignment with where the Moon is. The Earth physically expands (i.e. density decreases), both water and solid matter, during a full moon and a new moon, the times when the alignment is most exact. Scientists have measured this.

During eclipses, when the Sun, Moon and Earth form their most exact alignment, a noticeable increase in electron activity has been detected. What is detected is an increase in negative charge. Negative charge, which is negative potential energy, is an excess of energy in relation to the environment. The pressure from the Universe is decreased due to the increased blockage of energy by the Sun and the Moon. The same amount of energy is being emitted from the Earth, but the decrease in pressure from the Universe creates an excess (or at least more than usual) potential energy on the surface of our planet. The extra potential is observed as a negative charge and interpreted as electrons. (Electrons are a field of energy in reaction to an absence of energy that occurs when two or more spirals of energy intersect and decelerate.)

> Dan: "The planets do not add anything. They take away. That is the whole thing. What we see is the reaction, not the action. The planets are taking away potential energy because they are absorbing potential and converting it to matter. They filter energy. The matter they are producing from the energy they are sucking out of space is creating the shadow, or the effect of filtering energy. The Sun is drawing in energy from all directions, but there is a predominant suction line along the orbital plane. There are all kinds of planes but the orbital plane is the main resonant plane since it is tied into the Galactic center."[13]

---

[13] Conversations with Dan Dial. 1998 – 2001. My conversations with Dan Dial took place in Shelton, Washington between October 1999 and July 2001. Our sessions were recorded and transcribed. The quotes are direct quotes from these sessions. The explanations are my own and may or may not align with Dan Dial and his knowings.

The Planetary Effects on Earth and Humans

The human body and mind is the consciousness of the soul as it is expressed in this dimension — in this narrow band of spiral sizes and speeds, this narrow band of frequencies can be detected by humans in some way. The soul is expressed in many dimensions. The soul is a real, physical existence. It is a resonance or a series of resonances particular to a certain person, spirit or thing, particular to a certain manifestation that occurs in this dimension. Our bodies are the container, the expression of our soul as it manifests in this particular range of frequencies (which is the definition of this dimension).

All of us have a connection to other dimensions since we exist on other dimensions simultaneously. What differs in humans is the level of awareness of this connection. Why one person is more aware of this connection than another is somewhat complex. A variety of factors seem to play into it. In order to understand the factors we must understand the function of the emotions.

The emotions are a linking vibration between the physical body and the mental and spirit body. We know that emotions exist in this dimension. We can detect them from the effect they have. And though emotions constitute a range of spiral speeds and frequencies, they are in constant flux making it nearly impossible to measure. The emotions have a particular resonance that awakens the consciousness, allowing a connection between the body and spirit. Feelings are a way for us to tune in, to resonate with, to connect to, to become aware of the spirit.

All emotions can open the connection to spirit. Blocking emotion or feelings blocks the connection by shifting frequency out of phase. When a feeling is not blocked, the resonance occurs and an automatic connection to resonance on other dimensions (spirit, in some languages) occurs and the resonance shifts immediately. To try to hold onto an emotion once it has shifted is a way of blocking the present emotion.

There is a direct connection between the size and speed of the emotional and physical spirals. What is expressed in our physical body is directly linked to the emotional either through harmonics or through actual wave interaction and phase relationship.

Dan: "The planets create a shadow. The amount of energy it impedes versus what is flowing through it is infinitesimal. It simply adds a flavour to it, like a filter. It is altered. The larger Jovian planets are primarily gases so they do not block a lot of energy, but they block a large area. Mars, for instance, creates a more intense shadow because it is closer in proximity and it is solid rock. The Jovian planets [Jupiter, Saturn, Uranus and Neptune] are larger, lower density and are therefore altering the energy less but altering more of it."

Rosie: "If potential energy is bombarding the Earth from all over the Universe, wouldn't the energies that the planets are filtering be minimal?"
Dan: "That is true unless you take into consideration the minimal amount of energy that maintains the brain function. Brain energies are rated in millivolts per minute charges. Therefore, a minute charge variation or density variation from a shadow of a planet may seem small, (and it is as far as the general consensus of the environment is concerned), but not as far as our brain circuitry is involved. It alters its pattern. It does not discharge. If you change two lines of computer programming, you can throw the whole program off. It does not take a lot of energy to change the circuitry of the brain. There is a difference between the programming of the psyche and the physical psyche. With the physical psyche, we are all the same since we all come out of the earth, out of the human process of reproduction."

Rosie: "How is the psyche programmed and how does it connect with the planets?"

Dan: "The instant you come out of your mother's field is when the program is set. What were you aimed at? It is that point in the rotation. That is why birth time is so important. There is a mechanical physical part to astrology. It is not some nebulous spiritual thing. I have seen behavior patterns that are very specific to certain times of the year because it is not only the planetary effects but the galactic effects. What part of the galaxy we are facing makes a difference. There are all kinds of muddles of energy and shadows from all of those other solar systems and star systems. They are all involved."

The moment we take our first breath, we inhale our psyche, a field of energy that is in and around us. Until that point we are in our mother's field of energy. When we are physically separated from mother, then we can obtain our own energy field. It is within this energy field that the psyche's program is contained. The physical, the mental, the energetic, the emotional—all of these fields are interconnected.

The breath, ever so critical to physical life function, also is critical to the more subtle functions of the body. When we inhale we take in so much more than air. We inhale all of the potential energy present within our space. We inhale thoughts, emotions, radio waves and on and on. There is an infinite amount of potential energy available in the space in which we breathe. We also inhale the patterns of the Solar System. Currently, at the level of awareness of most humans, the solar system is the largest example of timing patterns that we can see and to which we can relate. While it will be wonderful when we can more completely plot the workings of the Universe and relate it to the events and patterns of our human lives, for now the Solar System will have to suffice. And suffice it does from my own experience. After exploring thousands of charts, there is no question in my mind as to the validity and corresponding nature of the planets to our psyches and personal lives.[14]

An Explanation of How and Why the Secondary Progressed Chart Works

This is a technique that has been used for hundreds of years. There is a general lack of understanding of how this works. It just works is what most astrologers know. Here I offer my ideas on the matter.

We are looking at cycles: the cycle of the Earth around the Sun (one year) and the cycle of the Earth moving around on its axis (one day). We have established numbers for these cycles (365 days/year) based on our connection to time. Let us for now call them cycles. A year cycle and a day cycle. Now let us make a leap: what if these two cycles are related, like a harmonic?

Imagine the Earth being created and sustained by a star which emits a ray of energy that intersects with a ray of energy from the Sun. Both the star (currently Polaris) or groups of stars and the Sun sustain the Earth's energy. The ray that is emitted from Polaris (or Vega or Thuban, depending on precession) is energy spiraling in a column fashion. The ray emitted from the Sun is spiraling in a planar fashion. The intersection of the two is then the orbit the Earth travels around the Sun in. The size of the orbit is one-year cycle that is a result of the size spiral and the distance that Polaris is from the Sun. The tilt of our planet points to the star that is sustaining us.

---

[14] Conversations with Dan Dial. 1998-2001

What creates the spinning motion of planets: Everything spirals. Both the cylinder and planar energies rotate. It is the interferences of the spirals that make everything rotate. It is the spirals as they go by one another that induce a spinning motion on the planet. That is what produces tornadoes, what produces planets. It is the spinning of that ball.

If indeed it is the interaction of the spirals that creates the spinning motion of the planets then, the same thing that is creating the orbital path is also creating the spin. Take the next leap with me. If both are created from the same interaction, wouldn't you think they would have something to do with each other — like a harmonic — or at least some reflection of each other — in time. A time harmonic.

If this is all so, then the progressed chart is a harmonic of the transit chart. From the date of birth, 30 times of the orbital cycle (years) equals 30 times of the spin cycle (days). Given that, then the progressed chart must tell us something about the cycle we are in. Maybe it is a focused image of the transit experience. Like a moment in time that is a harmonic of the time we accept as real time.

If in the moment that we are born, we are the Universe of that moment, then the progressed chart is who we are such and such years later.

Let us look at time. Spirals of energy are intersecting and moving in space all the time. In one space, say the space that our bodies take up, there are an infinite number of spirals moving and intersecting. What appears as matter in this particular space (say the space our physical body occupies) is an infinitesimal amount of the energy occurring in that space. The matter appears because a few of the spirals intersect in phase with each other, emit a spherical field that looks like an atom and interact with other atoms to form molecules. For the spirals to intersect and form matter in this dimension, they must not only be in phase with each other, they must also be of a certain size and slow enough in speed in order to register in this reality where an ear looks like an ear and a leg looks like a leg. Take those three factors into account: size, speed and phase plus the fact that the range of spiral sizes and speeds is a mere blip in the continuum of spiral sizes and speeds, then we are looking at the physical body as being a very, very small amount of the energy that occupies that space.

So what is all that other energy doing? Intersecting and not intersecting in other realms, in other time-space matrices, and in other perceived realities.

So what does this have to do with time? We need to think about time completely differently. Time as we usually perceive it is a linear and measurable function of distance, as if we can tick off years and minutes and days in our calendars. But this is not how time works. Time is a function of phase. The spirals intersecting in phase is what creates the moment we see.

Matter as physicists have been able to measure only occurs 10% or less of the time. Even saying 10% of the time is trying to make time a function of space. Really what they are saying is that there are multiple ways of experiencing time within the same space. Surely matter looks like it is always there, because of our perception. And so time is a function of perception, our ability to perceive. Clairvoyants and psychics have extended perceptual abilities. They step into other perceptions of time that is really other perceptions of the space. Our perception is related back to phase.

Most of us only perceive what is when we are "in phase" with what appears as matter in this dimension. In other words, we only perceive matter. This probably only takes up a small percentage of our brain power. What if the other part of our brain were there for us to be able to perceive other dimensions—the other spiral interactions that are occurring in the same space? Our eyes, while a fantastic tool for this range of spiral size and speeds, would be useless or used in a different way in other dimensions. If we opened up to greater perceptions, we would then be able to see time as a function of phase, of how much we are able to perceive in the moment. (Moment not being a measure of time but being a statement of is-ness, of the present.) The moment then could contain a lifetime of experience relative to our current and narrow perception. Like people who have near death experiences when so much happens and they have only been dead for minutes. They have stepped into greater perception, a perception outside of this dimension.

Appendix B: Cheat Sheet

SIGN		KEYWORDS	ELEMENT MODALITY	PLANET RULER		KEYWORD
Aries	♈	Uninhibited Rash	Fire Cardinal	Mars	♂	Instigation Will Force
Taurus	♉	Tenacious Stubborn	Earth Fixed	Venus	♀	Creativity Magnetism
Gemini	♊	Curious Scattered	Air Mutable	Mercury	☿	Thought Communication
Cancer	♋	Kind Emotional	Water Cardinal	Moon	☽	Feelings How we process
Leo	♌	Brave Egotistical	Fire Fixed	Sun	☉	Vitality Identity
Virgo	♍	Analytical Critical	Earth Mutable	Chiron	⚷	Healing Awakening
Libra	♎	Caring Indecisive	Air Cardinal	Venus	♀	Passion Love
Scorpio	♏	Honest Intense	Water Fixed	Pluto	♇	Transformation Power
Sagittarius	♐	Inspired Exaggerated	Fire Mutable	Jupiter	♃	Expansion Opportunities
Capricorn	♑	Organized Controlled	Earth Cardinal	Saturn	♄	Contraction Lessons
Aquarius	♒	Unique Aloof	Air Fixed	Uranus	♅	Sudden Change Awakening
Pisces	♓	Empathetic Sensitive	Water Mutable	Neptune	♆	Spirituality Vision

Appendix C: Different Forms of Astrology

1. **Electional**—sing astrological charts to choose a favorable time to do something (buy a house, get married)

2. **Horary**—erecting a chart for the moment that the question is asked and looking for the answer within that chart

3. **Mundane**—astrology of the world, applying astrology to understanding political and historical events

4. **Degree meanings**—usually based on the Sabian symbols which give each degree of the wheel (all 360 of them) a unique meaning

5. **Vedic Astrology** (Jyotisha)—astrology based on the ancient Vedic teachings used currently in India and getting more popular today—based on Hindu mythology and uses the Sidereal chart form

6. **Mythical**—interprets a chart based on the prevalent myths in the chart, often coming up with one personal myth per chart

7. **Humanistic**—interpretation of astrological charts that focuses on the person and allows for choice and free will:
    a. Purposive rather than deterministic
    b. A person's sensitivity is taken into account
    c. Holistic—the whole chart represents the person not just the sun or any single part
    d. Planets are given qualities that are human (anthropomorphic) instead of bodies as machines
    e. Creative power as crucial force.

8. **Medical**—emphasizes physical component to chart—uses signs, angles, houses, aspects to look into the physical body

9. **Esoteric**—usually based on the teachings transmitted by Alice Bailey and the theory of the Seven Rays. Incorporates different rulerships, i.e. Venus rules Gemini (traditional), while Mercury rules Gemini (esoteric), focuses on the ascendant as the spiritual purpose and integrates different definitions for the signs and planets.

Resources

Acker, Louis S. and Sakoian, Frances. *The Astrologer's Handbook*. Harper and Row Publishers, New York. 1973.
    A solid foundation in astrology. Somewhat old school. Easy to follow and read. Very clear.

Arroyo, Stephen. *Astrology, Psychology and the Four Elements*. CRCS Publications, CA. 1975
    A classic astrology text on the elements. He presents a depth that honors the individual and our free will.

Baker, Douglas. *Esoteric Astrology*. Baker Publications, Herts, England. 1998
Baker, Douglas. *Esoteric Astrology Part II*. Baker Publications, Herts, England. 1978
Baker, Douglas. *Esoteric Astrology Part VII*. Baker Publications, Herts, England. 1981
Baker, Douglas. *Esoteric Astrology Part VIII*. Baker Publications, Herts, England. 1982
Baker, Douglas. *Esoteric Healing Part III*. Baker Publications, Herts, England. 1984
    These are beautiful books filled with art and poetry — inspiring simply just to flip through the pages. Douglas Baker was a student of Alice Bailey's, pioneer of the Esoteric movement. He offers us an easy-to-understand look into the Esoteric world. However, the world still baffles me in many ways. These are not beginner books except for those who already have a foundation in the Esoteric way.

Bills, Rex E. *The Rulership Book*. AFA, 1971
    A fairly complete list of "things" that each of the planets, signs and houses rule. A must for Horary or Electional work.

Burt, Kathleen. *Archetypes of the Zodiac*. Llewellyn Publications, St. Paul, Minnesota. 1994.

Casey, Caroline W. *Making the Gods Work for You*. Random House, NY. 1998.
    A thoroughly enjoyable read that describes each of the planets complete with stories from her travels, anecdotes from everyday life and many quotes and interesting stories from famous people. Without knowing anything about astrology you can pick this book up and enjoy it. She does talk about the Saturn return. She does not talk about house and sign positions of the planets.

Clow, Barbara Hand. *Liquid Light of Sex*. Bear and Company Publishing, Santa Fe, NM. 1991.
    By one of my favorite authors, this book is a classic for astrologers and those completely new to the field. She talks about various life transitions including the Saturn return and the Uranus opposition that happens at around age 40.

Donath, Emma Belle. *Asteroids in the Birth Chart*. AFA, Tempe, AZ. 1979.

George, Demetra with Bloch, Douglas. *Asteroid Goddesses*. ACS Publications, San Diego, CA. 1986.
    The classic text on the major asteroids and some of the minor ones.

George, Demetra. *Finding Our Way through the Dark*. ACS Publications, San Diego, CA. 1995.
    Demetra George is a pioneer in the use of the asteroids. I love her ability to connect mythology and interpretation.

Gillespie, Sally and River, Lindsay. *The Knot of Time, Astrology and the Female Experience*. Harper & Row, Publishers, New York. 1987.
    This book has an excellent history of astrology and insightful interpretations of the signs.

Green, Jeffrey Wolf. *Pluto I*. Llewellyn Publications, St. Paul, Minnesota. 1985.
Green, Jeffrey Wolf. *Pluto II*. Llewellyn Publications, St. Paul, Minnesota. 1997.
    Two books that take us on a journey into the depths of Pluto. Very important books in my library. Not necessarily written for the beginner, but not prohibitive either. These are the foundation books for his work which he calls "evolutionary astrology". His work is pivotal in the changes that are happening with astrology today.

Greene, Liz. *Saturn: A New Look at an Old Devil*. Samuel Weiser, Inc., York Beach, Maine. 1976.
    This is a classic text by one of the most respected astrologers in the world. She does not talk about the Saturn return or Saturn transits but focuses on understanding Saturn in our natal charts, an important piece to the Saturn return.

Guttman, Ariel and Johnson, Kenneth. *Mythic Astrology: Archetypal Powers in the Horoscope*. Llewellyn Publications, St. Paul, Minn. 1993.

Hone, Margaret E. *The Modern Text Book of Astrology*. L.N. Fowler and Co., London. 1951.
    An old-story, classic textbook. It is easy to reference for the facts of astrology. I find things in her book that are hard to find elsewhere.

Kochunas, Bradley W. "Returning Soul to Astrology". *The Mountain Astrologer*, Aug./Sept. 1996, pg. 18-22

Lintner, Anita. *Astrology Practitioner Course.* Home Study University, CA. 1994.

Millard MD, Margaret. *Casenotes of a Medical Astrologer.* Samuel Weiser, York Beach, ME. 1980.

Nauman, Eileen. *Medical Astrology.* Blue Turtle Publishing Cottonwood, AZ. 1993.

Oken, Alan. *Alan Oken's Complete Astrology.* Bantam Books, NY. 1980.
    This is truly one of the most complete astrology books I have ever seen. If there was a companion book to my wok, here, it would be this one. While at times the material can be dense, I always learn something new — every time I open the book. While this book is about exoteric or traditional astrology, Alan Oken's depth of understanding the esoteric models comes through. This is not an ordinary astrology book. Do not let the title fool you.

Plumb, Mary. "Geoffrey Cornelius, On Divination and the Roots of Astrology", *The Mountain Astrologer*, Oct./Nov. 1996.

Rudhyar, Dane. *The Astrological Houses.* CRCS Publications, CA. 1972.

Schulman, Martin. *Karmic Astrology: the Moon's Nodes and Reincarnation, Volume I.* Samuel Weiser Inc., York Beach, Maine. 1975.

Seymour, P.A.H. *Astrology: The Evidence of Science* (revised and extended paperback version), Great Britain: Arkana-Penguin, 1990.

Spiller, Jan. *Astrology for the Soul.* Bantam Books, USA. 1997.
    A wonderful book for anyone interested in their soul's journey.

Starck, Marcia. *Healing with Astrology.* The Crossing Press, Freedom, CA. 1997.
    She explores herbs, aromatherapy, foods, flower essences, gems, colors, sound, etc. and the relationship between these and astrology. An herbalist and an astrologer, she writes clearly and consciously about both.

Other non-astrology resources:

on gem stones:
Melody. *Love is in the Earth.* Earth-Love Publishing House, Wheat Ridge, CO. 1995.
    The most complete book on gem stones around and one with which I consistently resonate.

Peschek-Bohmer, Flora and Schreiber, Gisela. *Healing Crystals and Gemstones: From Amethyst to Zircon.* Konecky & Konecky, old Saybrook, CT. 2002. (English translation, 2003)

on flower essences:
Kaminski, Patricia and Katz, Richard. *Flower Essence Repertory.* Earth-Spirit, Inc., Nevada, CA. 1994.
    The book on flower essences, nothing else compares.

McIntyre, Anne. *Flower Power.* Henry Holt and Company, NY, NY. 1996.

on aromatherapy:
Aromatherapy: *A Complete Guide to the Healing Art* by Kathi Keville and Mindy Green
    While there are many excellent books on aromatherapy, this is one of my favorites.

Glossary

Astrological chart = A picture of the sky. The main components of the chart are the planets which are each in a sign and in a house.

Horoscope = the interpretation of the astrological chart

Each chart has 360 degrees.
Each sign has 30 degrees of the circle.
Planets in their signs are placed in one of the 360 degrees.
Each house has a varying number of degrees depending on the house system you use. (In the Placidus house system the number of degrees in a house is dependent on the longitude and latitude. Houses and signs do not have to agree. In fact they often do not agree in the Placidus house system.)

Zodiac - The division of the sky into sections called signs. There are two types:
1. **Tropical** - This one is used most commonly in the West. It divides the sky into 12 equal sections of 30 degrees. Each section corresponds to a sign. The beginning of the tropical zodiac is the Spring Equinox. On that day the Sun rises at the beginning of the Zodiac sign of Aries.
2. **Sidereal** - This is used mostly in Vedic astrology that comes from India. This system has continued the practice of the signs corresponding to the constellations.

Ascendant (ASC) = rising sign= represents your personality, your physical presence in the world, how you see the world and how the world sees you. The lens through which you view the world and the world views you. Starts the chart with the first house.
Imum Coeli (IC) = roots; foundation; base; traditions; movement toward earth; Mother Earth; inner reality
Descendant (DSC)= begins 7th house; represents the Other; mirrors of ourselves; reflections
Mid Heaven or **Medium Coeli** (MC) = begins the 10th house; our path in the world; our work; our walk in life; Father Sky; outer reality; movement toward sky.

Transit - "A transit occurs whenever a planet, moving in its orbit during our lifetime, forms an aspect to a planet in our natal horoscope." Robert Hand
A transit expresses times that are appropriate for certain kinds of actions.
Transits indicate how the symbolism of your life unfolds in time, exactly as do progressions. While transits give greater detail over the short range, the progressions indicate a more general structure over a longer time span.

Secondary Progression = derived by equating one day for each year in a person's life
- expresses inner changes, experiences and movements. There is debate among astrologers that the progressions often are expressed externally as well and can be used to look at timing of events.

Solar Arc Direction = uses the arc of the Sun's movement in one day to determine the degree of movement and then applies this degree to all planets. Expresses timing of events—usually used to predict world events—also used in personal charts to predict events and look at energies that are being affective and effected much in the same way as progressions and transits.

Glossary

Solar Return = the solar return chart is used to observe the energies available for the year, the themes of the year ahead, and the struggles and fortunes of the upcoming year for an individual, a nation, a business or anything that has a birth date. The chart is calculated by taking the exact degree of the sun in the birth chart and drawing up a chart for the particular time that the sun is that degree for the year to be looked at. The sun will always be at the same degree as in the birth chart and every other planet will be different since it is a different year.

Rulership = each sign has a given ruler — the planet ruling the sign can offer more information about how that sign operates. Each house has a sign that rules over it as shown on the cusp. Look to the planet that rules that sign for information about that house.

Retrograde and Direct = the motion of the planets in the sky. Retrograde is when a planet in relationship to the Earth appears to be moving backwards. Direct is the forward motion of the planets in relationship to the Earth.

Ecliptic = the orbital plane of the Sun, the plane in which the planets orbit.

Orb = number of degree variation allowed for a particular aspect or transit.

Cusp = the degree of the zodiac that separates one house from another

Planets = the energy, the characters
Signs = how the energy manifests
Houses = in what area of life the energy manifests
Aspects = the relationship between the energies

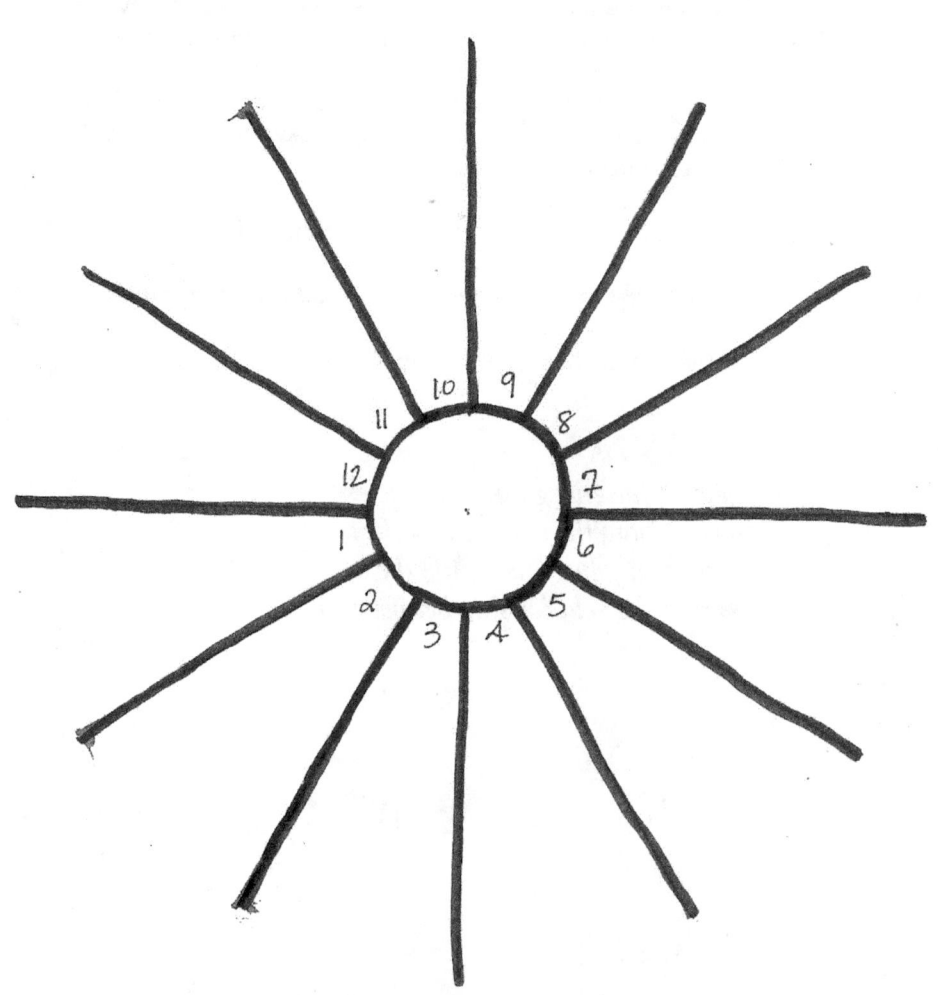

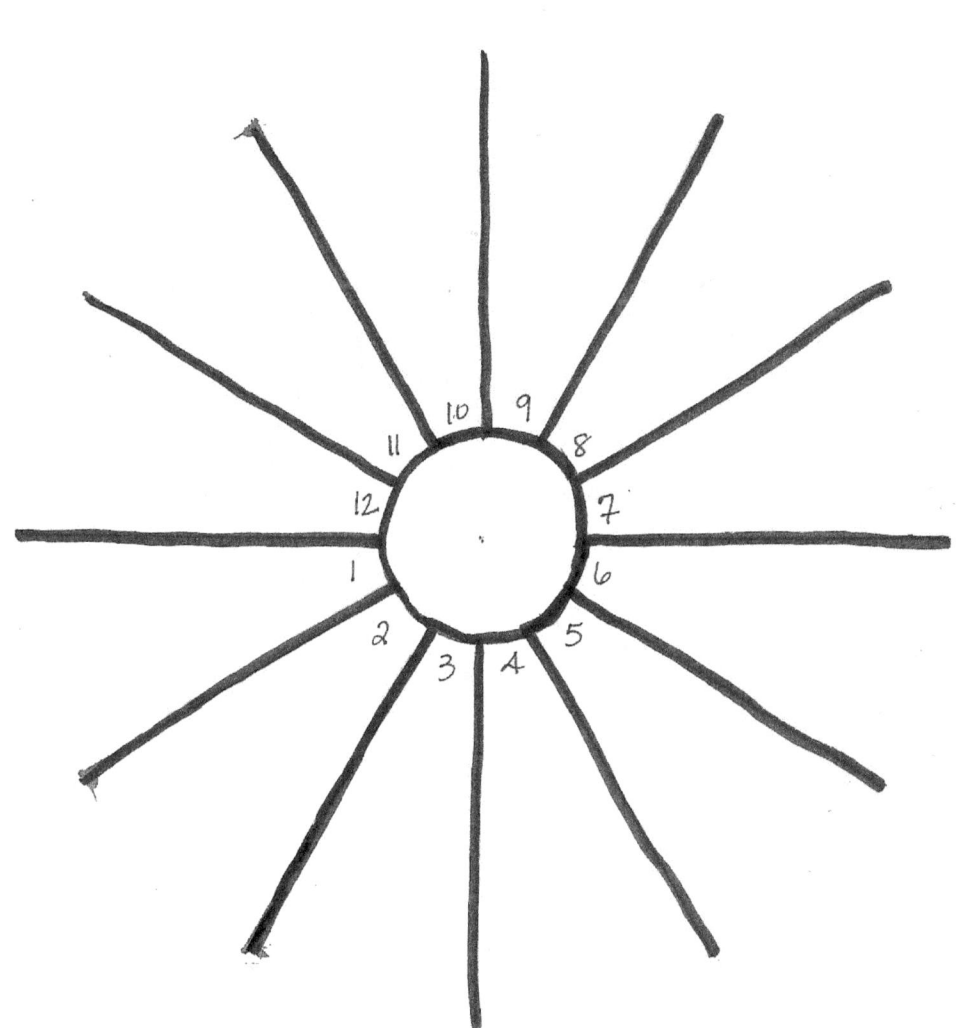

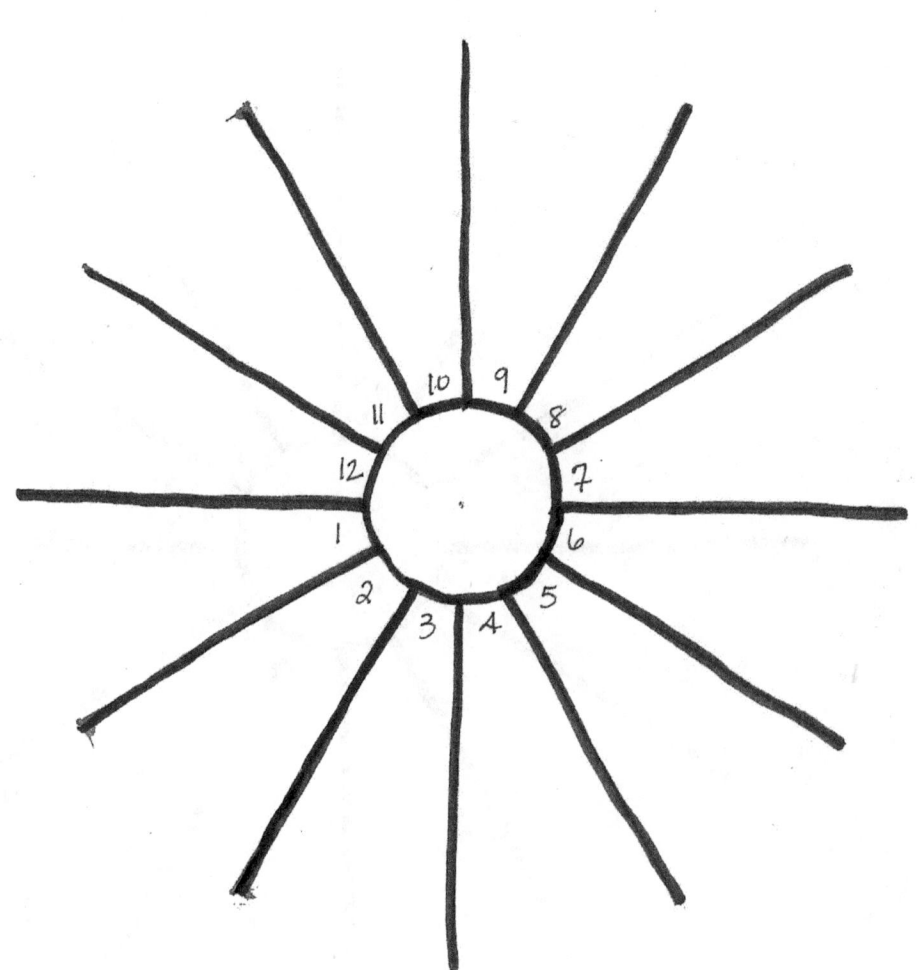

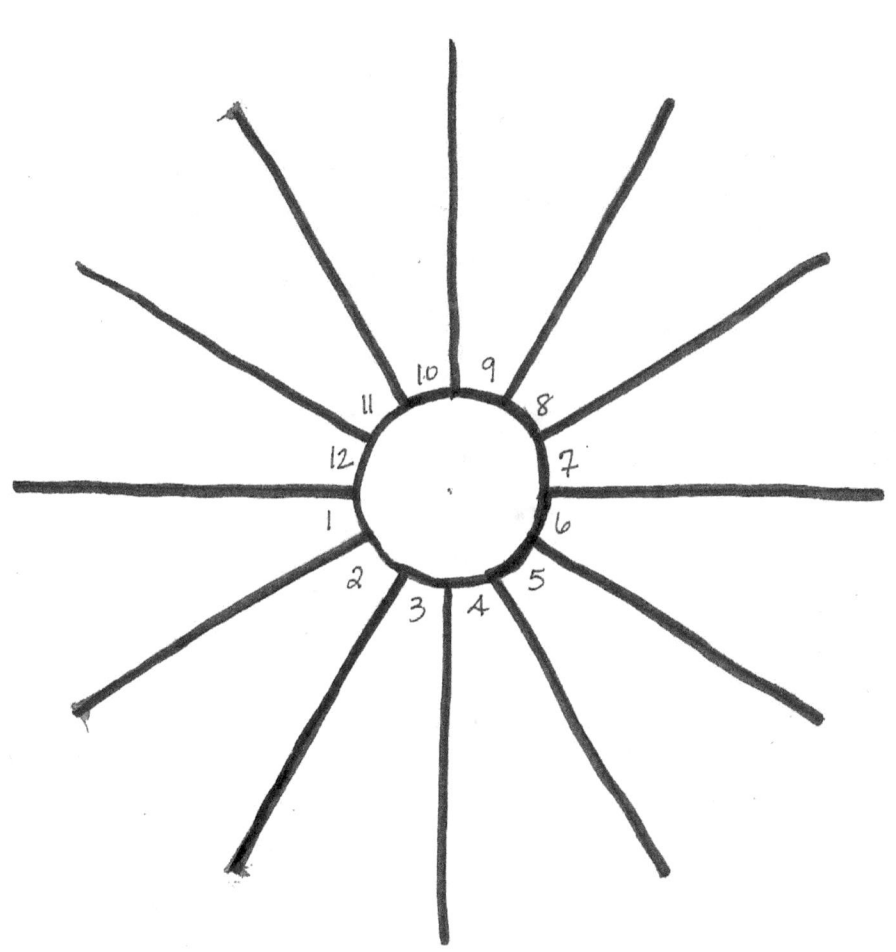

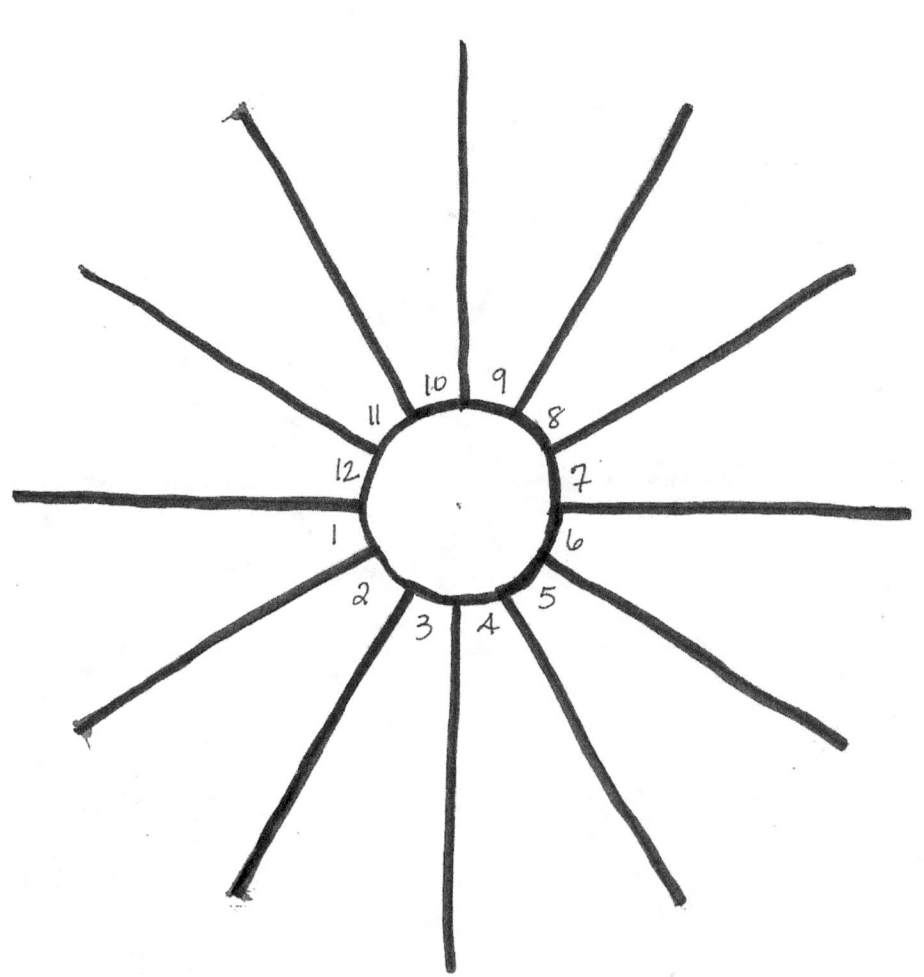

www.ingramcontent.com/pod-product-compliance
Lightning Source LLC
Chambersburg PA
CBHW080513110426
42742CB00017B/3096